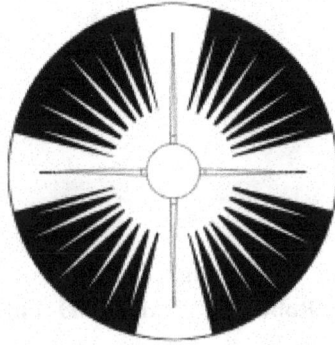

THE
ROBERT
COLLECTION

Including:
Serving Littleness
Anthology of Love
The Voice Within
Legend of Turtle Feather
The Fool's Journey

Robert M. Waldon, ND, PhD

Reunion Press
17664 Greenridge Road
Hidden Valley Lake, CA95467
(800) 919-2392

ISBN: 978-0-9899133-6-2

This collection is a gift to myself and to those who read all or part of it. My desire is to share important parts of my journey in the hopes of awakening and inspiring others to do the same.
I invite you to celebrate the gift of who you are.

Robert

INDEX

About This Work

This is not a chronological offering, but an inspirational one.

Serving Littleness was written on January 28, 2007 at a time when I was examining what we have been taught, both individually and as a nation, that it was appropriate, even necessary, to help the weak and needy.

Anthology of Love is a collection of poems I wrote while spending a week in silence at a Vedanta Retreat in Marin County, California in 1985. This was a time of major transition and turned out to be the precursor to a dramatic focusing of my life purpose.

The Voice Within is the earliest of the included writings in this volume, being written during a specific period of time between September 28 and October 12, 1980. These were my spiritual questions, directed to what some might call my Higher Self, and the answers I was aware of at that time. While I experience less separation between my self and my Self than I did at that time, this was a profound developing spiritual understanding.

The Legend of Turtle Feather is a short piece I wrote on a 7 day Vision Quest in the mountains of Northern California in September of 2001. There were 10 of us gathered for the Vision Quest and, unknown to us at the time, we exited our ceremonial circle to go our separate ways at the exact time of the bombing of the first Tower in New York on "9/11". We knew nothing, consciously, about what had happened until we left the wilderness a week later and saw our first newspaper.

The Fool's Journey was a piece I wrote in 1997 as I was exploring the relationship and progression of the major arcana cards in the Tarot. I have always appreciated the symbology of the Tarot, the I Ching and other "esoteric" games, which allows us to project our current condition or experience onto something seemingly external to us in order to come to a deeper understanding or our life.

These writings serve as my reminders and as my gift to you.

Serving
Littleness

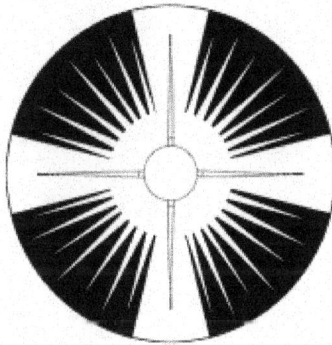

Robert M. Waldon, ND, PhD

Robert Waldon, PhD, ND

Serving Littleness

What if it's true that we have built our world around responding to and serving neediness, littleness, lack and pain? That appears to be the way it is. That is not the way of Nature. Nature supports the strong and fit and resourceful. The mind of man has developed (and expressed) the ability to interfere with the natural way. We began by using the mind as another tool or resource for survival. The problem came in when trust fell out. No other animal kills when it is not hungry in order to store up for later. That is symptomatic of the many ways we have used our mind and our clever creativity to handle our lack of trust.

Most species respond in a manner consistent with the survival and well being of the species. In man, selfishness has become an issue. There is a focus on survival of the individual over survival of the species—seeing ourselves as separate from the whole. From that came guilt. In our recognition that we were out of balance or off purpose combined with a belief that our fears, insecurities and lack of trust were based in reality, we experienced guilt, rather than a return to Truth.

Guilt appears to be nothing more than a recognition that we have made a mistake combined with an unwillingness to choose again or to see things differently. Because we could no longer trust God to protect us (from ourselves), we began attempting to expiate our guilt by selectively taking care of those we were hurting. It seems "logical" that the strong, living in fear, would not take care of others who were also strong because that would increase the threat to themselves. The only place we could "safely" express our need for atonement would be on the weak—those who could get better and stronger enough to make us feel good, but not so strong as to threaten or challenge us. The position of "power" then became weakness which played on and manipulated guilt, but never let itself appear strong enough be threatening.

This probably plays out in each of our lives, with most of us playing both roles at varying times and to varying degrees. We come into this world "strong"—happy, whole and free— which threatens those around us. Those who are not totally inculturated very early on are at least taught not to be "selfish", but to take care of those who have less (usually our "teachers" themselves wanting something from us). Eventually, the world around us conspires to break us down in some way, in some arena, and that is where we get hooked in the game.

Once we become hurt or needy, usually finding no help or support, we begin to believe that being whole can hurt others (because we believe ourselves hurt) and we make sure never to do that to ourselves or to others. We also begin to take care of the needy in hopes that, if we are ever needy again, we will be taken care of. "There, but for the grace of God, go I" is a powerful statement of gratitude as well as a powerful link in the chain that binds us to the world.

As a result of these experiences and choices, we trust less in God and others, focus more on taking care of ourselves, and operate to handle fear rather than to extend love. We seek to be strong more for the purpose of not being needy, rather than because it is our natural state. We offer "alms to the poor" as our bargain with the universe to protect us.

We have developed a culture which worships rising to greatness by overcoming adversity. The stronger or more painful the adversity overcome, the more we worship. There is the insane belief that those who have suffered much and attained, will be more kind, understanding and generous to those who still suffer much. The easier and more natural the expression of wholeness and power, the more we distrust and attack and attempt to defeat or overthrow.

We now have a world where more suffering creates more safety and support, and where the harder you have had to work and the more you have had to overcome, the less vulnerable you are to attack.

That's why forgiveness is a threat, both to the one currently suffering and the one who has overcome. If forgiveness is real, there is no excuse to suffer, and there will be an instant return to self-responsibility. And, if forgiveness is real, there is nothing that was ever really overcome, which leaves the now happy and healthy at the mercy of an attacking world.

Our work is to forgive and live, not condemn and die. It's the old dilemma of who lays down their arms first and, "can you trust enough to be that vulnerable?" This is the stuff of martyrs. They did the right and noble thing and the other guys not only did not lay down arms, but attacked. That's the glue-story that holds the old paradigm together. Whenever we reach this point of recognizing the game and being able and willing to choose for Truth, we remember, or are reminded of, those who went before on this same path and the price they paid.

We need to stop glorifying the martyr and stop projecting our own experience on the stories of the saints. We need to know, even more clearly and strongly, that nothing real can be threatened. It is only our belief in pain and suffering that creates those experiences in us and creates our perception of those experiences in others. Somehow, we need to call the game and not allow ourselves to be hurt.

When I believe in this whole worldly drama, I want to die. That's the only logical conclusion to the scenario. Some die sooner, some later. Some die happier, some in more pain. Some leave simply and quietly, some suffer. Each of those vignettes is glorified by some religion, or sect or group. It matters not. The result is always the same—death.

The more I affirm eternal life, my right to fully live, the more it seems that life, the world and my body create challenges, as if to say, "How dare you question (threaten) the established order of this world? Believe in all of this and see the error of your ways." My experiences then, represent my internal conflict about what is really true. I notice that I begin "working hard" at living as a denial of death, rather than just being fully alive.

In those times when I have just been alive, caught up in a moment of joy or love or creativity, I transcend the pain and suffering as well as the reward and success, and experience a taste of eternal life as it was given to us by our creator. The mind says (and, therefore, proves) that we can't live like that forever. The truth is that is the only way we <u>can</u> live forever. It is also, quite probably, the only way we would be <u>willing</u> to live forever.

Who could bear the thought of eternal life as an extension of how we have mostly experienced life in this world? Most of our choices and experiences in this world are tolerable only because they have an end. Until we choose for love and forgiveness as our only response and our entire focus of being, the concept of time will remain to protect us from experiencing an eternity of hell. When we no longer make temporary or expedient choices, time will cease to exist and death will be an unnecessary concept.

Until then, how do we best live? Choose for joy and a life of serving love. Support those who appear to need no worldly support with your love, your joyful thoughts, with trust and freedom. Remember that God's will for you is perfect happiness and choose accordingly. Let go of using "stories". Let go of growth and development and working on it. Stop searching for enlightenment and let it dawn on you. Resist not evil or error, but rejoice in the light. Where the sun shines, there is no darkness.

From the **Tao of Robert**:

How is it that the little limit the great?
The slow outpace the swift?
The weak defeat the strong?
The empty cup,
Having a hole at its base,
Can drain the fullest vessel.
The rains do not delay
To give slow farmers time to plant.
Winter does not wait
To protect late-maturing fruit.
The flowing river,
Upon reaching a precipice,
Does not consider the earth below before plunging over.
The sun rises
Even if men still sleep.
Thus, the wise man waits for no one
And serves all.

What do we do with physical discomfort and pain? Notice it and refuse to use it as a tool or an excuse to either get what we want or to avoid what we don't want. Respond with attention to the body when it becomes a distraction and use that call to love yourself and offer love to those with whom you interact. Find ways to let the truth be known that this call is a gift so that you can affirm the truth for yourself and your world. As much as possible, move through the inconvenience, choosing for love and joy, doing what you are called to do—what has heart and meaning—giving yourself to your world.

Physical, mental or emotional pain are all signs of being off purpose. You must be willing to let go of all you have been holding dear which is actually holding you in fear. Pain is an insistent call to imagine (image within) a life so full of joy and so on purpose that we would be willing to live it forever. Although it is much harder to imagine that world than it is to hold the mistaken images you have adopted, it is much easier to live that life than it is to continue your current struggle for existence.

What if we were to simply change our minds and move our lives back on purpose? In addition to separating ourselves from the rest of our world and setting ourselves up for attack, there is also the part of the mind which judges ourselves for the foolishness of apparently wasted time and for being so stupid as to have believed in the illusion for as long as we did. The internal threat to our peace and safety is more potentially damning than the external threats (knowing that our internal states create our perception of external reality).

There is no true forgiveness which does not include the erasure of the mind. Anything even dimly remembered is not forgiven. The only true and complete healing is the state where there is no memory of ever not being healed and whole. You cannot both forgive and remember. You cannot both fully trust and still protect yourself in some way. You cannot wholly know the truth and still believe in any part of the illusion. You cannot be totally free in only part of your life.

It is like a bird in flight. In order for flight to occur, the earth must be left behind. For many, the leap of faith is frightening and life threatening. For those who know and trust their ability to fly free, it is exhilarating. Just as most baby birds need to be initially pushed from the nest for their first flight, so we use the world to push us into our own experience of our "moment of truth". Where we differ from birds and the natural order is in the use of our minds. Our mind is potentially the greatest tool for freedom and it is also the biggest block to responding to the call for freedom when it comes. The bird, knowing nothing else, instinctively opens its wings and flies. Human beings, knowing too much else, override instinct and block the God-given, natural ability to soar above the illusion and experience freedom. In our choice to see ourselves as victim, we crash and burn.

Because the power of love which created us may be occluded, but cannot be overcome by the world of illusion, we rise again—Phoenix-like—with the opportunity to choose again, to see things differently, to forgive ourselves and our self-created illusion and return to our natural state.

Sometimes, in our inability to totally forgive, we cannot let go of feeling hurt. Forgetting is a form of temporary forgiveness. Since death is a form of both denial and forgetting, we choose to "die" in an attempt to start over with a clean slate. We move, leave relationships, change jobs and even physically die. We give ourselves repeated opportunities to get enough momentum in the direction of truth so that we can easily spot and overcome error when it presents itself. It is said "Denial is a powerful protective device. You can and should deny that error can hurt you." (ACIM)

Because death never really changes anything, we will ultimately be faced with that which we thought we left behind. Hopefully, we have grown stronger in our remembrance and recognition of the truth so that we can really let go the next time. We will ultimately succeed because no illusion can hide the truth in us forever. We will ultimately forgive all of our mistaken perceptions and return to love. We can forgive now or we can forgive in a later now. It is all the same, in truth, but it is a very different experience in time. The earlier in time we forgive, the sooner we return to joy and an experience of life we are willing to have be eternal. We can choose to be happy pioneers, leading the way for our world ("Forgive now, avoid the rush.") or we can choose to hang on to our misery a little longer yet, until forgiveness is more in vogue and appears to be easier.

Forgiveness opens us to the experience of being willing to once again give freely of ourselves ("Life is forgiving and you are the gift.") and to recognize and fully receive the abundant gifts being presented to us in every moment.

Robert Waldon, PhD, ND

From the **Tao of Robert**:

Water poured into an empty vessel
Greatly depletes its source
Before fullness is achieved.
The greater the emptiness,
The greater the danger to the source.
Water poured into a full vessel
Overflows immediately to good cause,
Bringing fullness to those also served
Without depleting the source.
The greater the fullness
The greater the joy to the source
And the greater the good to all.
The wise man
Knows to serve the mighty
So all whom they also touch are served.
To serve the weak
Encourages and supports weakness.
The great lake neither dries up nor empties
Because it is constantly renewed.
Many rivers bring it life.
It is open to fully giving
Because it fully receives.

Anthology
of Love

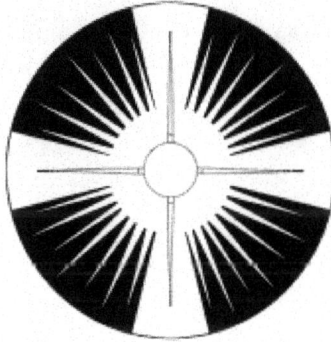

Robert M. Waldon, ND, PhD

Robert Waldon, PhD, ND

The World I See

The world I see
I know full well
For I have created it
And it is wholly mine.

Whether I accept this fact,
In this moment,
Or would renounce my creativity
And ascribe all power to one outside myself,
The reality of Truth is undeniable.

I judge my world, and I am stuck,
Forever lost in the illusion of Good and Bad,
Light and Dark, Time and Space,
When all there is, is love,
And all that blinds me to its omnipresence
Is my fearful thought
That somehow I must die.

Arise

Arise and brightly shine
You holy Son of God
In whom the world is whole
And with whom angels sing.
Accept the love you are
And know the truth of your creation,
Free of sin and error,
Free of fear and pain,
Born of love,
Forever love to be.

No longer lost in the illusion,
I truly see the world
That God, through me, created.
And it is good.

A Moment

For just a brief moment
Forget who you are
Forget all your fears and your burning desires
Forget all your past, any guilt you are bearing,
And remember the pure love of God.

For just a brief moment
Remember your dreams
Remember all hopes and your high aspirations.
Remember to savor each moment you're given
And bask in the light of God's love.

You're a child of that light
A Son of the universe
Beloved of God, full of hope for the earth.
You're the giver of love to a world which is needy.
You're the presence of God among men.

Forget not your birth
As a spirit of holiness.
Remember your part in this drama called life.
The river of peace leads us all ever homeward.
Look into each life and see there a friend.

Fear not for your actions,
Be they perfect or flawed,
For the judgment you render is purely your own.
Each act is of holiness, leading us upward,
Inexorably home to the bosom of God.

Love

Love
That very essence of our being
The power of creation,
without which all creation would cease.
The one abundant, truly free commodity in this world
The infinite, never-ending, undeniable statement
Of the presence of God
Love
In our anxiety to live our own, separate lives,
We often lose sigh of it.
We translate our divine longing
To earthly ideals which we think more easily attained.
In our mental separation
from the very Source of our being,
We lose our ability to create true love.
We sometimes despair
For love
God's perfect gift, from which we were born.
He never leaves us as we sometimes leave Him.
Love knows no separation,
just as separation knows no love.
By His grace, we are ever welcomed home
We are ever sought out by God,
Even in the midst of actions we may consider unholy,
In His divine desire
To fulfill our own, sometimes hidden, divine desire
To bring us back home
To love.

Today

Today, while the moment still lives,
We choose.
Those yesterdays which make up our past
Are history,
An integral part of our being,
Defining us, but not limiting us,
Setting the stage, but not the script.
Tomorrow is the world we create
With our thought,
The picture we paint
On a canvas prepared
By choice, circumstance and divine decree.
Nothing immutable, unchangeable or beyond our control
Wince we wield the brush,
We hold the palate in our hand
Within the hand of God.
We are creator.
And when we touch that divine spark
Deep within the core of our being
And bring to life its blazing crystal light,
We know our true inheritance
We clearly see our mission
And cause the light and love of God
To manifest on earth.

Open My Eyes

Open my eyes to the world around me.
Not the world of illusion and chaos
But the world of love which underlies all.
Open my eyes to freedom

Help me to see, not the mistakes and problems,
But the perfection behind every action,
The lesson in every decision,
Which brings us closer to God.

Help me, not to forgive,
But to understand that no forgiveness is needed
For self or for others
When we see through the eyes of love.

Let me live in a way that speaks love
To all whom I daily perceive
That we might forever grow closer
In the recognition of our common goal.

For we all seek but one thing—
Reunion with Self and with God.
In the recognition of that fact, together,
Is the open road to freedom.

The Gift of Peace

Peace I give to you
Not as an answer or tool,
But as a gift of love
To support you in times of need.

Wisdom, ever new,
Is ready upon request
To answer your every need
As you go through this play of life.

Strength I lend to do
That which you have chosen,
To accomplish what you will
From the silent depth of your being.

For nothing stays the same,
Each piece affects the whole.
Each thought creates a pattern
Which moves you to your goal.

So let go and let it be.
Know perfection patterns all.
Be ever active as you're led
To answer your life's call.

Give freely of yourself.
All gifts come from above.
For all there is was given you
In God's gift of perfect love.

One With The Infinite

Know that you are one with the Infinite
That it need only be perceived by you to be true.
Know also that you are one with all who surround you
And with all souls everywhere.
There is no order of magnitude,
No greater or lesser,
There is only God.

Know that to make this reality known to the world
You must give of yourself, you must share love.
Know also that in that sharing is growth and expansion
That all souls everywhere,
Regardless of current awareness,
May experience love
And know that they are God.

Know that in sharing, we find ourselves and our purposes.
In giving, we fill our own lives with God's holy grace.
Know also that in helping others to see their own paths
We are given the light we need
To travel the path we choose.
For there is but one path,
There is only God.

Know that in love there is unconditional peace
Regardless of all that may shake our world.
Know also that love is all there is.
All else is a lie.
And lies build the traps
From which love sets us free.
Step forward to God
And share the magic of love.

Freedom

The world
Is not our adversary.
It is not God's plan to thwart our goals.

Those demons
Which we so bravely battle
Are the products of our own dreams and fears.

Fears crying
To be set free, released
From the captivity in which we hold them.

And when released,
Transformed into the nothingness
From which they were first created

Leaving us free,
Free to fully inherit
Our legacy of God's perfect love.

Living The Presence

Love
Soaring on eagles' wings
Dancing wit the clouds
Playing with the stars
And sending its message of strength.

Love's light
Beaming down from the heavens
Shining brightly through the skies
A promise of salvation
Radiating to earth's very core.

Love's messengers
Walking everyday streets
Leading everyday lives
Winning and losing and growing
And living the presence of God.

Love's Song

Love's song
Calls sweetly to my ears
Leading me
Enticing me
Gently
Into the presence of God.

Love's voice
Speaks bravely in my heart
Encouraging
Strengthening
Giving courage
To be the presence of God.

Love's note
Rings loudly in all men
Sounding
Resounding
The message
We all are the essence of God.

Go Forth

Go forth
Into a world of your making
Into the circumstances which you have chosen
For your soul's growth.
Meet that world with strength and assurance.
And in those moments when you falter
Find your strength in love.

Live life
In the fullness of its glory
Accepting the perfection of each experience
As it moves you onward.
Trust in the guidance you've been given.
And in those moments you know doubt
Find your strength in love.

Share joy
In each soul which touches yours
Giving what peace your heart can offer
Knowing it is enough.
Experience the gifts you're given.
And in those moments when you hunger
Find sustenance in love.

Love That Overcomes

That love which overcomes,
Not by strength in bearing arms,
Nor by cunning or stealth.
That love which recognizes no conflict
Which acknowledges no winning or losing
But ever affirms the oneness
Which finds each one of us
To each other
And to our God.

So give love
To every person you encounter.
Know the spreading glow of glory
That comes therefrom.
Know God is in each gift.
And in those moments you believe
Find your life in love.

Light and Life

Light and life
Inseparable gifts from God
Known fully to those who scour the heavens
And plumb the deepest depths within
In search of that love
Which sets them free.

Searching, reaching,
Ever expanding
Never ending co-creation
Knowing the world is not a trap,
But our road to freedom
Filled with the opportunities to learn
From the choices we have made.
Filled also with friends
From our sol's journey
Here to support
And strengthen
And guide
That we might never be alone.
A life of love in its truest sense
In that every action
Perfects not only ourselves
But all whom we love.
And knowing that love
As the true love of God
Perfects all creation.

Fill Me

Lord
Fill my life with joy
That I may experience with wonder and enthusiasm
The world we together have prepared
As my arena for growth.

Fill my heart with peace
That I may grow from the calm acceptance
Of the fruits of my every actin
And know their perfection.

Fill my mind with challenge.
Let my petty ego stand against Thy will
So that I may learn to choose
And recognize the truth.

Fill my soul with love
That I may know all souls as one with Thee
And therefore have no reason
To see myself alone.

Rejoice

Rejoice
For the time is now
When we can know the truth
When we can acknowledge our rightful place
At the hand of God.

Sing the song of love
That touches the very hearts of men
So they may know God's presence
And worship Him within.

Give the gift of love
That the deepest part of man
May overflow with its abundance
And transform the world.

Trust the power of love
Which brought us to this world
That we might learn to rightly chose
And know the love of God.

Live a life of love
A life of such devotion
That so perfectly mirrors God's presence
That all mean shall be set free.

The Power of God

The power of God
Flows through us
Cleansing
Creating
Changing

That transformational force
Applied by God through self
So that, in the end,
We might know
The source of our strength,
The truth that makes us one,
That every deed
Changes every soul.

We may act in that light
To change our lives and our world
And know
The power of God.

The Strength of Love

The strength of love
Softly cradles the soul
Providing a safe haven
From doubt and fear.
It opens the heart
To the music of angels
Clearing a channel
For the voice of God.

It starts with caring,
A clear recollection
Of purposes shared,
God's work to be done.
The depth of communion
Brings all souls together
Giving light to a world
Where darkness prevailed.

The light of God's promise
Shines brightly within us.
Our primary task
Is to let it be seen.
For a glimpse of that light
Re-kindles the purpose
Reaching out to all souls
To awaken God's love.

To Touch God

To love
Is to touch God
And in that touch
To find ourselves transformed,
Never more the same
Ever more one
With the ultimate Source,
And apparent object,
Of that love.

Truth

Truth, as we know it,
Binds us to our sense-born world.
Truth, as experienced through God,
Sets us free from earthly limitations
Dissolving all illusion
Removing every lie
So, truly, we can see,
In every soul, our self
And in our self, see God.

The Source of Love

God
The source and object of true love
Seen in the face of every person met
The true essence of each earthly soul.
That presence, unseen, which guides us
By the voice which sounds
just below our conscious thought
Is God
Creator of the universe
The power behind the stars which light our sky
Life force of all creation
Existent in every rock and tree and flower
That power of nature that draws from us its recognition
As God
The salvation of our world
The oneness which, when seen, unites
And brings true happiness to life.
No more the unaffected "I"
Ever more the healing recognition
We are God.

True Love

True love
Knows no bounds or limitations
Not selecting just the best
But seeing in those darkest spots
The perfection of creation
Which is God.

True love
Accepts that part of self
Which we despise in others
As perfect for the moment
To bring us back together
As one in God.

True love
Sets us ever free.

Forgive

Be open to forgive
Release your love, free as the air
Which flows from place to place
Perfect for the moment
Unseen by any
Giving life to all
Neither yours to withhold nor to give
But yours to share.

Recognize the truth
That all your dreams are your own
And all your hopes are of vanity
Until that perfect moment,
Unforeseen and unexplained,
When you touch the very heart of God
And know His love.

Let the power of love
Spread from deep within our heart
To touch all souls on earth and everywhere
That all may one again affirm
The truth that we a re free
Unchained from bonds of individuality
And one with God.

Listen

Find the moment in which you can listen.
Give whatever you must
Put aside all you think is important
Take the time to be still in God.
For those things which we value are nothing,
The precious thoughts we cling to are lies.
All truth resides in God's perfect love
From which we create a new world.

It is only our fear that holds us back,
Only our desire for the familiar.
It is our uncertainty that things can be perfect
Which blinds us to the transforming power of love.

For we must let go in order to move on.
It is not a safe step, but a leap
In which we must totally break contact
To find our lives transformed.

Find the moment in which you can listen.
Experience the power of God's love.
Let His light ever shine from within you
And touch the souls of men.
For the lack of a model can hinder
Not knowing what truly can be.
Be that leader, believer and guide.
Be God's gift of love for the world.

Touch

The world has touched us
And left its mark, be sure.
For never can we travel this path
And remain unaffected, unchanged.
It is what we do with our chance,
How we master the challenge,
That determines our growth.

For Go has touched us
And left His mark evermore.
He has made us creator
To fashion the world of our dreams.
And it is that world we create,
From the strength of soul's purpose,
Which is the mirror of His love.

Remember

Remember
Those moments
When happiness filled your heart
When joy so filled your world
That you could not help but share it with others.

Those moments
When peace and tranquility
Created that perfect bubble
Insulating you from the distractions of a busy world.

Remember
The sureness
With which you saw clearly
The road that opened before you
Removing all doubts as you travelled your path.
The souls with whom you shared love
With no thought of self or receiving,
But only of sharing and giving the strength to grow.

Remember
Those moments
You were clearly one with God.

The Voice

Clearly sounds a voice
Above the din
Above the noise and disturbance.
It is the voice of love
Piercing the veil of delusion
Bringing joy
True hope and fulfillment
In the promise of peace.

From whence comes that voice?
From lips, it seems,
Of a stranger.
From the embrace of a friend.
In the sound of a breeze
Softly blowing
Lightly touching
Caressing the soul.
From a thousand thousand
Seeming sources
Each touching us
In their own way
And yet, not one is truly acting
Individually, alone.
Each voice we hear,
Striking love's harmonious chords
Deep within our soul,
Is but the voice of God
Calling to His own.

Be Still

Be still
And know the fullness of peace
Calmly acting
From strength which grows
Out of the depths of silence.
Recognize the power of being centered in love,
The ability
To give, and not be needy
To fee, and not be hungry
To support, and not be weakened.
Know the endless bounty
Of God's giving
Ever filling the cup
Which has been emptied in His service
Clearly showing the way
To those who lead His beloved children home.
It cannot be done by you
But that He will do for you tenfold.
For that is the true message
Of God's love
Which is bestowed upon us,
And, though us,
Upon the world.

Peace

Peace I find,
Not in the mere absence of conflict
Or in the avoidance of discord.
For peace is not a static thing
To exist in some protected void
Sheltered from the world.
But rather Peace
Is found within the world
Amid the turmoil of everyday life
In the natural give and take
Of human relationships
Growing out of the love of God,
And the love for God,
Which recognizes all men as brothers
And each experience as perfect,
Ideal for soul's growth.
The calm loving acceptance
Of that which is,
Knowing it is of God
And knowing that those agents
Of supposed discord and strife
Are His children,
Working His miracles of transformation
On our lives.
Only in truly recognizing God's plan
And the perfection of His will
In the dynamic and total
Loving acceptance
Of all God's children in their chosen roles,
Can we carry the message of that love
And know true peace.

Searching

Long have I roamed
Through the regions of earth
Over hills
And in valleys
On the mountains of solitude
In my never ending quest
For God's elusive love.

Restlessly I searched
Through the lives of mortal men
For some clue
Some hint of that hidden path
Which would lead me to my goal
Of blissful rejuvenation
Found in His presence.

Then in final desperation
I scoured the regions of my soul
Only to find
The simple truth
That what I so valiantly sought
Was already mine
Ready and waiting
Needing only my simple acceptance
To transform my life.

Thy Presence

For Thy love, oh God,
Working through my life
And reaching out to touch the souls of men
I am truly thankful
For, in being Thy instrument,
I am double blessed.

Keep my heart ever open to Thy voice
That I may benefit from Thy wisdom
Keep Thy will clearly obvious before me
So that my human will
Might ever recognize the surer path
And ace as Thy agent.

Open my soul to Thy peace
As I travel my path homeward to Thee
That I may ever draw strength
From Thy presence within me.

Live In Peace

Live in peace
Without effort or strain.
For discordance results
From trying too much
And allowing too little.
Rather than acting upon
Our own interpretation
Of the will of God
Let us allow His will
To work itself,
Through us,
And see our actions
As the perfect expression.
Learning therefrom.

When it no longer matters
What form the outcome,
Or how His love is expressed,
Then the perfect realization
Of His will in our lives
Will clearly manifest
And lead us home.

When we step out of the way
God can work through.
When we squarely face the light
Unashamed, unafraid
All darkness falls behind us
And we are filled
With the love of God.

Too Many Times

Too many times
I have forgotten.
Too often
Failed to forgive,
Both self and others.
I have lived
Too much of the earth
And the time has come
For change.

Soul is aware
Of a greater truth,
Of the eternal
Unyielding
Never ending
Forgiveness of love.
Aware of a purpose
Transcending earthly limitations.
Born to rise above conditions chosen
And light the way
For peace.

In clear recognition
Of the Godhead
Within,
Each seemingly separate soul
Can rejoice
And sing
And dance
To the music of creation

Which we,
Together,
Have written
And in which we,
Together once more,
Will be fulfilled.

Thoughts

Our thoughts
Are the forerunners of creation
Attracting to them
The energy of divine manifestation
Which knows neither good
Nor evil,
Only being.

Guide thou our thoughts
Oh God,
That they be in Thy image
Forever
To fulfill soul's purpose
Bringing love and peace
To reality within the hearts of men
And firmly establishing
Thy holy presence
In our lives.

Floating

Floating
In the sea of spirit
Safely cradled
In divine love.
Rising high
On the crests of expectancy.
Feeling
Momentarily
Alone and set apart
But ever returning,
With great joy,
To that creative oneness
From which we came.
Washing softly
Over the sands of experience
The grains of which,
Too numerous to count,
Are worn to smoothness
Over time,
Losing all capacity
To further irritate the soul.
Never truly separate
As we,
With increasing certainty
Come at last to recognize
This ocean of eternal bliss
As our beloved creator
And our Self.

Open Your Heart

Open your heart
To the message of God's love
For that alone
Will bring you peace, fulfillment and healing
Through the reaffirmation and manifestation
Of soul's purpose on earth.

None can teach us
Or be taught by us.
We all but help each other,
Through the experiences of our lives,
To reach the threshold
Of our inner knowing.

There, we may re-discover those truths
Which are the essential cornerstones
Of our being.
And in the re-awakening
Of that knowledge stored within
We find true healing
Of body, mind and spirit
Arising from the awareness of oneness
From whence we first came
And toward which we travel
As our final destination.

Footsteps

Follow the footsteps
Of the great ones who have gone before,
Masters who have led the way
And brought to the world
God's gift of love.

Only human, yes,
But transformed by that love
Into a greater humanity,
Into that which we all are destined to become
As children of God.
Freely giving that gift
Of unconditional love
To the best of our ability and understanding
At each moment,
Ever growing through the use of that gift and giving
To the greater understanding
Of our purpose in life,
Of God's perfect will,
And His infinite love.

Laughter

Find once again
The joy of laughter
And peaceful repose.
Listen for the melody
Of love's perfect song
Brought to our hearts
On the wings of divine friendship.

The perfect mirror of God
Shows His face in all things
Hoping to remind and succor
Those searching souls
Who diligently walk His path.

Until that perfect instant
When we are ready to recognize the true source
Of all which we so ardently desire
God will fill our lives
With as much of His loving presence
As we can possibly accept
At any one moment.

Hold to those moments
Like pieces of a sacred puzzle
For when the truth of the emerging picture
Becomes undeniably clear
We are free.

Live For God

Live for yourself and for God.
Let others follow the paths of their own desires.
Be not bound
To the pleasure of things
Or the fear of what they may do,
For that will ever hold you
In the world as you know it now.

Rather
Be free.
Feel the perfection which is you
Regardless of earthly conditions.
Know that no gain or achievement,
No answer found in materiality,
Its abundance of lack,
Can affect the perfect peace
In your soul.

It is only a lie
Which can hold us captive,
Believing that what we do or have
Can in any way change who we are.
Until we see the truth
We will not be free.

The love of God
And the abundance that is His
Is the legacy that awaits
Our recognition of who we are
And from whence we came.

Each New Day

Start each day anew.
Greet the dawn with an open heart
And with words of love on your lips.
Know that each new day is a miracle
Hoping to happen
Ready to change your consciousness
And your world
All the love and the power and the beauty
Which is God
Comes with you
To acknowledge the perfection of your actions.
All the pain and anger and negativity
Which is a lie
Must be physically brought
As unwanted burdens
Which create the stumbling blocks
To your spiritual progress.
Choose not to bring the pain
For that choice is your birthright.
Choose not to bring negativity to you day
But allow the pure love of God
To wash over you
Cleansing body, mind and soul
Opening your life
To the unfolding miracle
Of you.

Imagine

Imagine
That all you hold dear
Is suddenly taken.
All your possessions,
Your wealth and your power,
Your family and friends,
Even health,
Is denied you.
Your whole world is shaken
With no place for shelter
Nowhere to turn
But to God.

We've lived this before
To teach us this lesson
And will live it again
Until it is learned.
For God is the source
Of all wealth and power,
The presence we love
In family and friends.

As long as we see Him
Ours is the universe
With no need to fear
Deprivation or loss.
All is perfection
When God's will is guiding.
Clear is the path
When we walk by His side.
Nothing else makes us whole
But His love.

Live Life

Live life to the fullest.
Feel vibrations of love
Permeate the core of your being.
Hear the resonance of OM,
God's eternal note of creation,
Resounding through your world.
Find sustenance for the soul
In holy communion with God
Transmuting all that enters your life
Into that perfect image
Of Him with whom we are truly one.

Life itself is but a play,
A catechism we repeat
Until the lesson,
In all its subtleties and implications,
Is perfectly learned
And we allow ourselves to move on.

Resist not the role
For it was not imposed or assigned
But chosen by Self,
In moments of attunement with Spirit,
As that perfect lesson
To advance us on our path.

Celebrate life.
Celebrate that role we call self
And acknowledge the sanctity and perfection
Of your being
Which is God.

Love Sets You Free

From the bondage of fear
Uncertainty
Unrest
Love sets you free.
In your need for sustenance
In body
Or spirit
Love is your endless supply.
In your search for friends
To share your path
Love opens the door.

Love is the tool
Sufficient to every need
The answer to every desire.
For, in true love,
We dwell in that holy relationship
With the Master of all things,
The designer
Creator
Provider
Of all that is
Or shall be.
The richness of that treasure
Is never denied
To those who allow self
To freely partake,
Openly share,
And know no separation from
God's love.

Experience God

Give love
And experience God.
Know what it is to be blessed
By the outpouring of His love
From every corner of your world.
Accept that love
And in so doing
All those who act for God
In loving you
Are blessed.

Live in this dynamic fullness
Of love's encompassing power
And know that you are free.
Know that you know God.

Spirit

Spirit
Ever living
Ever new
Creating worlds to experience
Within the mind of God
To reawaken that part of Him
Which is us.

Guidance

So often
We forget to ask
For guidance
Reassurance
And love.
Then, our comfort lies
In that paltry support
That we,
Acting alone,
Can provide self.

Far better
To open our hearts,
To bare our souls,
And admit
To the weakness experienced
By limited ego.
To ask
For all which is rightfully ours
As sons and daughters
Of Father/Mother God
Whose endless bounty
Sustains us always
Limited only by our perception
And willingness to accept.
For in asking,
We allow ourselves to receive
And in receiving,
We cannot help but share
The overflowing bounty of our gifts
In answer to the prayers

Of others who also ask.
Those who accept love
Will love.
Those who experience love
Will know God.

Speak

Speak
With the language of the heart
For where words fail
Love will surely be sufficient.
When anger threatens,
Open up to that forgiveness
Which recognizes each soul as Self
And each lesson as a gift.
Where sadness breaks,
Find healing in remembrance
Of soul's purpose here on earth.
Listen also,
With the heart,
That God's sure message of salvation
From our self-imposed estrangement
Will not go unheeded and the healing power of love,
Expressed within our lives
May unite us
With every seeking soul
That we may once again
Be free.

Give Love

To give love
Is to be blessed
By the omnipresence of God
Who first loved us
And who uses us,
When we allow,
As His instrument for spreading love
On earth.

To receive love from another
Is to acknowledge that power,
That universal creative force,
In which we are all united
As children of God.
Without that recognition
Of shared sonship with our creator
We remove ourselves
From the transforming radiance
Of God's perfect love.

We live our lives always
Within a vast ocean of cosmic bliss
Surrounded ever
By the power to create and transform
Entire universes.
Yet we can still choose
To cut ourselves off
And drift under our own ego direction.

Rather
We should choose life with God
Acknowledging the fact,
Which will inevitably be
The essence of all we come to know,
That we are God
And need not suffer loneliness
Deprivation or need
Except by our own choice
To learn that simple truth.

Lose Your Self

Daily turn your life to God.
Feel His presence every hour
Find the strength to move ahead
In His creative power.

Move not upon your own resolve
Without attuning first
To the love directing every step
And quenching every thirst.

What we build of self is lost to us.
Trust yourself and you will fail.
But lose yourself in love and find
That being Him is all.

Beyond

From beyond the dimension of time
The hand of God
Reaches out to touch us,
To hold us
And to bring us home to Him.

From beyond the confines of material creation
The love of God
Penetrates our heart
Reawakening the sleeping soul within
To shatter forever
The illusive dream
In which we,
Temporarily,
Allow ourselves to believe
That we could possible be anything
Which is not truly God.

From just beyond the limits
Of our imagination
He whispers to us
The truth that we are He.
And finally,
We hear
And we are free.

Know Love

God
The changeless
Formless power
Behind the ever-changing
Form of His creation.
The essence of,
Yet not limited to,
The world of materiality
Which so defines
Our daily experience.

Know His love
Coming from beyond,
Extending to beyond
The limits of the universe we know,
Bearing with it
The power to create anew
Or re-create
The pattern of our lives
And bring us home again
To the realization
Of our oneness with Him.

Seeking

The limits of experience are such
That they bring us to the door
Which opens up eternity,
But cannot serve
To see us to our final destination.

For the world of experience
Is built upon desire
Which leads us through a maze
Confused by unfulfilling emulation
Of true creative ability
And unlimited abundance
Which comes from God alone.

We must seek until we find
That our love for God
Outweighs the rest.
For that love alone
Can cast aside all doubt,
Remove all shadowy imposters
And unlock that final door
Through which we again become
He whom we have sought.

Freedom

Freedom
That illusive ideal
For which we search in daily life
And worldly endeavor,
That mis-directed desire
To exercise our will
And impose it on the universe.
That which, while we so ardently seek,
Eludes us.

For freedom,
Which would profit self alone,
Cannot be found.
Only love,
Encompassing all,
Acknowledging our roles
As instruments of a greater will,
Can set us free
And bring us home,
A family of man,
As children of God.

Stillness

Still the rushing waters of the soul
That God's face may be clearly reflected.

Calm the turbulent winds of the mind
And know the stillness of eternal peace.

In doing,
We establish our relationship with the world
And accomplish what lessons are to be learned.

In being,
Keeping centered in the heart of love,
We establish our relationship with the infinite
And know God,
Gathering the strength to do,
The vision to see,
And the wisdom to know
Even the minutest details of this sojourn
And the purpose for which we have come.

Hear The Song

Hear the song
See the light
Feel the love
And experience life.
Come to know God.

Born of Light

Born of light
In darkness descended
To more fully know that light
When our eyes once more are open.

The Presence of God

Seeking
Searching
Concentrating on the presence of God.
Sometimes fighting
With earthly patterns of our mind
In an effort to focus on the path.

Frustrating at times
Until we recognize
That God can move mountains
So we don't have to.
He can change the course of rivers
And place stars in heaven.
So, of course,
He can alter the pattern of our lives
And orchestrate events
To bring us home to Him.

Our part
Is but to listen
And follow that sometimes quiet voice
Which says "You can."
To have that tiniest bit of faith
Which opens our hearts
To the transforming power
Of His love.

Be ever vigilant,
For the kingdom of God
Is manifest for you.

In Times of Crisis

In those times of crisis
When turbulence seeks to overturn
That fragile stability
We seek so vainly to maintain,
We must ever remember
That change brings truth
To those who hear its words.

Transformation is the only way to God.
Whatever we are, imagine or hope to be,
We are but ever-moving particles
In the universal consciousness,
Gradually increasing in awareness
Of our ever-present divinity.
We move only by choice.
Nothing happens but by divine decree
That we may grow enough
To know ourselves as God.

Know Love

Know love
Free of all emotions
For emotions are born of the flesh;
Without attachments,
For they, by their very nature,
Hold us;
Without will or decision
Which place constraints
And artificial boundaries
On that which is boundless.

Accept God's love
In all its manifestations.
Whether
In our current, limited perspective,
Events seem good or ill,
They are of God
Working in us and through us
And they are appropriate.

Perfect love
By removing self
And allowing Spirit to manifest,
Responding to the Son of God
Which is every soul we meet;
Willing to accept
From whatever person, source or event
The lesson that we are one in God

Despite this temporary condition
Of individuality
Which tempts the ego
To stand on its own.

Know that love is the key
Unlocking the door
Allowing us to individuate
From these conditions of life
Which hold us separate from God,
Not to deny,
But to rise above
Encompassing these experiences
In the greater knowledge
That we are free to be God
The moment we allows His love
To freely flow through us.

The Stillness

Through the stillness of life
We pass.
Unsure, but not unknowing
On a path who's end we do not see,
Though the landmarks are sometimes familiar.
We travel not alone,
But with friends
Some of whom we meet for the first time,
Most of whom we meet again
With some vague sense of recognition
Or a clear and instant rapport
Which surprises both of us,
At first.

Events,
Deliberately drawn to us
And known by the experienced traveller
To be planned by us as well,
Crowd in upon the stillness
And threaten to unbalance the tranquility
Which is our birthright.

In time,
We come to recognize
The limitations of our earthly thoughts
Which visions peace in terms of those events
Which do or do not occur around our being.
Then we begin to see
That, if we could find progress
Through the experience of tranquility,
Devoid of all challenge and stimulation,

We would not need this earthly incarnation
At all.
We could rise upon the winds of heaven
Back to the heart of God
And that would be sufficient.

But there is more.
How easy to resist temptation
When it does not exist.
How easy to love God most
When there is no alternative.
And how shallow and weak the devotion
Which has never made a difficult choice
Or, God forbid, a mistake.

To Dream

To dream
Is to awaken that part of us
Which never really sleeps,
But which we fail to fully see
In our pre-occupation with worldly cares.

Our dreams
Are our creations
Seen by us first
Before manifestation
In form and substance.
The prelude to that
Which takes us sometimes unaware
Because we fail to understand dreams
As the cornerstones of reality.

All men fill their sleep with dreams
But wise men see those dreams
As markers on their path
Leading them,
Most surely and swiftly,
Into the presence of God.

By Choice

So, finally, we come to know
That we are where we are
By choice
And by divine decree
That we might be given another chance
To choose
And to know the consequence of that choosing.

It is not to suffer,
Though some elect that path.
It is to experience
And to come to the sure and certain knowledge
That the quality of that experience
Is determined by perception,
How we, as individual beings,
Choose to respond.
It is the peace within
Which brings us home to God.

Enter The Light

Enter into the light.
Dare to let each darkened corner of your life
Be exposed.
Look into the light
And see that which you have feared
Dissipate and wash away.
It is the darkness of your fear
Which holds you,
Which keeps those hidden places
Festering and in pain.

In truth, there is no hiding place,
No place where who you are is not seen and known
By you and by God.
There is no place untouchable by love,
If you allow yourself to be healed.
There is no need to perpetuate the lie of sin
If we trust in the love of God.

We only hold onto what we hate in ourselves
To make us right in our mortality,
To prove that we either deserve or cannot escape.
While all along,
The perfection of our immortality
Proves that we are fee.
There is no world which can hold us,
No limits which can define us
Except those we place on ourselves.

So enter the light
By opening your mind and your heart
To its eternal presence.
Cleanse yourself of all that is not real
So that you may once again enjoy your own company
And welcome the company of God.

Imperfections

Do not attack your imperfections
For they are merely occluded perception.
Be perfect
By acknowledging your perfection.
Accept all of the past
Which has brought you,
And all of the future
Which has led you,
As the perfection you are
For having created
The eternal now
Which you can experience.

Our Direction

Where have we lost our sense of direction,
Our reason for being, the plans we have drawn?
Why do we fear for the outcome tomorrow?
Do we really wander alone?

For we've left not the garden of truth and of beauty
Never a step have we gone from our home.
We know that we live in the light of Thy presence
So why do we feel so alone?

And then we awaken as if from a nightmare
To find that we never have left what we've known.
It's all a delusion, something we have created.
We've never been really alone.

Just sometimes we choose to live in the shadows
To look at the void, to explore the unknown
For a moment forgetting it's all an illusion
Overwhelmed by the feeling of being alone.

We know that we need to experience the shadows
Learn to be in, but not of, what we're shown
To walk through the dream secure in the knowledge
That no one is ever alone.

No one can be, whether waking or dreaming,
Other that one of God's own.
It is we who forget, never He who forgets us
For He love us too much to leave us alone.

Surrender

Unchartered seas beckon us,
Frighten us some,
But draw us inexorably forward
To re-discover those parts of Self
We have hidden away
In the mistaken thought
That we are of this world.

And so we go forth,
Ever seeking for direction and guidance,
Never quite sure of the path we have taken
Until that pivotal moment in our existence
When we no longer choose,
When we no longer decide the path
But allow ourselves to be led
By that part of Self
Which is our ever-present
And direct connection with God.

We find ourselves through surrender.
Not a surrender of Giving up,
But a surrender of acknowledgement,
Recognizing the ultimate source
Of power and light in this universe,
And seeing our true function
As beacons
To bring that light into our world.

The Voice of Your Heart

Be still
And know great peace.

Hear, perhaps for the first time in a long time,
The voice of your heart
Leading you
Where the voice of your mind
Would never go, nor dare to follow.

See clearly the path that lies before you
Knowing it starts exactly where you are.
It has no past of relevance
Except that it brought you to this place.
It has no set direction
Except that defined by where you turn.

Be still
And know that where you quest
And what you seek
Is not reached by outward journeys.
Rather, follow the path of soul
Which leads within,
A path which begins and ends
With you.
A journey of a thousand miles
Or a thousand thousand years
Which can be traversed
In a single moment of transformation
Upon recognition that where we are going
Is where we are.

Be still
And know thyself.
Be still
And know God.

Heal Yourself

Heal yourself of pain and sorrow
Making whole once again
The truth of your being.
Bring balance to your life
So perspective is maintained
And your mission is fulfilled.
Then look to others with whom you share
And recognize their struggles
Are yours as well
For you have seen them as part of you
And invited them into your life.
Provide the space for healing
In body, mind and spirit
So they too may be whole once again.
And then believe the truth
That all men are your brothers
And therefore part of you in God.
Extend your love
That they may know its healing peace
And walk once more in light.
The world will change,
A total transformation.
First recognize your own perfection
Then don't deny one part of God's creation
As being part of you.

Know Joy

I looked upon the blossom
Radiant in the morning light
And I knew joy.
For the beauty of that moment
Touched my very soul
And brought music to my heart.

Gently my mind remembered
The barren ground of winter,
preceding fruitful spring,
When nothing here stood
But rock and earth,
And I knew sorrow
At the lost beauty of the moment.

Quickly, my mind proceeded
To the scorching suns of summer
When gentle leaves of color
Lay scorched in mid-day's glare
And I knew fear,
For I did not wish to lose
The loveliness possessed.

Quietly, I looked around me
At the glory of the blossom,
Seeds sown in barren winter,
Leaves transformed to summer soil,
And knew the magic of the moment
Was the love that touched my soul.
The one thing never changing,
Never missing, never lost

Is the love of God,
Born deep within our being,
Which creates perfection
And makes each second
A holy instant in which to live.

As I look upon each moment
With no remembrance and no fear,
I see my life as perfect,
Born in the light of love.

Born In Light

Be born again in light.
Trust in the light
That you will need no defense,
For the love of God
Does not acknowledge attack.
Become fearless
Knowing that who you really are
Is immortal
And incapable of being damaged or changed.
Judge not
Lest you turn yourself
From the true vision of God.
Forgive not
For it is unnecessary
If you do not first condemn.
Learn from the past,
Acknowledge
Accept
Enjoy and release it
For otherwise it will not release you.
Anticipate the future.
Look forward to being,
But do not forget to be
Here and now.
Live each moment
For therein lies the experience of eternity.
All that ever was or will be
Is present now
To be fully experienced.
Do not attack God
By denying your perfection.

See Myself

At times I see myself,
Not recognizing who I am.
Acting strangely,
Different from the norm.
It's as if I see
Some old, long hidden part of me
Rise to the fore
In outright challenge
Of who I think I am.
The choice to me is clear,
To deal with what I see
Or bury it anew.
In either case, I change.
To face with strength and vision
Brings growth
While denial brings weakness
Born of opportunity lost.
In moments, I am healed.
Forever transformed
By the gift of this freedom.
I bow in open gratitude
To my friend
For having been the mirror
Reflecting my inner fears
That I might melt them away
In the light of God's l

Robert Waldon, PhD, ND

The Voice Within

Preface

These words are written as a message to him through whom we speak, but contain a truth for all.

Know, all who read these words, that wherever you see truth, we have spoken directly to you.

Wherever you feel love, we have shared love directly with you.

Wherever you feel touched, we have laid our hands directly on you, wherever you feel these words are spoken to you, know that it is truth.

To all who read these words in the spirit of love and with a desire for understanding, know that we speak them directly to you for the greater glorification of God, through you.

Patience

September 20, 1980 7:30 AM

This morning our lesson is on patience.

Strength comes through position, and position is established by patience. Even as the butterfly flies from place to place, it has beauty and grace, but no strength. There are those things in life whose goals are beauty and grace and, to that end, they may flit from place to place. But strength of character must be established by the persistent confrontation of ideals and a firm rooting in situations created for ourselves. The tree has great strength grown from this firm rooting and constancy in facing the elements surrounding it.

You are to be as the walking tree, able to move from place to place, staying long enough to become firmly rooted and grow from interactions with the elements in each new surrounding, gaining strength at each stop.

However, and this is where patience plays, you must be wise enough to extract maximum growth from each step before moving on or vital lessons will be missed. Never fear or worry, just recognize why it is you feel "stuck" at times in time or place. Mobility must be maintained, but strength must be nurtured. We will guide you and clear your path at each step so nothing will be lost in your passing.

This is patience.

Humility

September 20, 1980 8:15 AM

Humility grows also from strength developed by patience. Humility is the recognition that yours is not the great accomplishment, merely the fulfilling of a commitment already mad to yourself and the world.

Does a man feel pride if he can lift more than a boy can? No, a man recognizes that he possesses greater strength and maturity and, therefore, ought to be able to life more. There is no pride in besting an inferior in an unequal match. There is joy only in accomplishing that which one sets out to do. With that joy, comes the recognition that we did this, not ourselves, but had many hands and hearts at our service.

Therefore. Be humble that others may gain proper experience from the recognition that great deeds do not swell your head. See that they are not intimidated from pursuing their best efforts in life by a foolish earthly pride, but that they recognize that we are all brothers in our striving for growth. Our strength lies, not in separatist pride, but in humble assistance one to another, even as we assist you in our way.

Sin

September 21, 1980 9:05 PM

There is no sin in the eyes of God. Only Man knows sin. Man's belief in sin has created sin, and the dire effects those actions considered sinful have upon him.

God knows only action in whatever form it may take. Experience is the key and the reason for our being— experience and growth through knowledge born of choice, free choice, by each one of us. Man, in his desire to magnify his importance and falsely magnify the significance of his every action, has taken it upon himself to judge others. In so judging, man finds himself at the point of cause (creator) and others at effect (created), which imparts a false sense of power and importance. God, Himself, is truly Creator and each of us are creators **only** to the degree that we manifest God within ourselves and let God's love shine through us.

Man has created a trap by his considerations of cause and effect and the weight of importance he has given them. When he finds himself judged, by either himself or others, he immediately becomes effect and, therefore, no longer in control of his own destiny.

Since man's ego still strives to protect its petty importance, he must assume that a higher power has placed him in this predicament of being judged, and therefore falsely accuses God of passing judgment and being vengeful. Know that **this is not true**. Man's actions are his own and the predicaments in which he finds himself are of his own choosing and devising. These lessons are the ones he has chosen to learn and—listen to this well—he will not fully learn them until he recognizes they are of his own choosing and not discriminatorily visited upon him by some outside power or force.

Man's only "sin" is the failure to learn and to grow through the experience of his choices. But, even this "sin" is an impossibility of existence, since man **will** learn and **will** grow. Be not mistaken. There is no consideration of time for the Almighty. It exists only in the mid of man to serve as a measure, a yardstick, to crate a condition of progress which man can relate to. For many, tis is not necessary any longer. There is no past, present, future. Man just **is** now. Upon proper realization of this simple fact, there is no progress, as you think of it now, in steps, one at a time. There is an explosion of growth through experiencing, in a fuller sense, that which we know on an intellectual or soulful level.

Man's limitations create sin. Recognize that those things we do in life involving others (and everything we do involves many, many others, both on the physical and spiritual planes) are done for the mutual experience and consequent growth of all people involved. A person would no be involved in not of his own choosing. There is no right and wrong, in the greater sense. There is only action and experience. Right and wrong, like time, merely serve as a measuring rod against which to view certain of our actions.

All is in the experience. The same actions may be experienced against a variety of "moral" backdrops, through a series of incarnations, before the soul has completely integrated that set of experiences into its being. The experience of eating meat is very different in, say, India and the United States. What is the absolute truth on the question of eating meat? The truth is that which provides for growth and progress of the soul.

Lest we begin to sound as if your actions don't matter at all, or that you may "eat, drink and be merry", do not be misled. You have goals and purposes and it is our progress toward the realization of these against which the should measures itself. You, yourself, would not tolerate long the wasting of a lifetime's opportunity to progress. The greater goal toward which you strive is of utmost importance to you—much on the order of magnitude in which your physical bing craves air, water and food. You will not stand long to be deprived of any on of these, if it be in your power to prevent it. The key to this all is that it **is** in your power. All is in your power and all will be accomplished all **is** accomplished, by you.

It is your desire to grow and serve your higher self, you impatience to be accomplished, that leads to the creation of concepts of sin and good and evil in your temporary blindness to the true oneness of us all in God's love.

Silence

September 22, 1980 3:20 AM

"To know, to dare, to do, and to be silent." The motto of the Great White Brotherhood. In silence comes the fulfillment of your goal, the true knowledge that what you did was pleasing in the eyes of God and that acknowledgment on the earthly plane is not only superfluous, but would be demeaning to the true value of the action. Silence acknowledges your acceptance of the omnipotence and omniscience of your God wherein all that is done, is known. Silence acknowledges your ability to recognize right action on your own path and to allow others the right to their own conceptions and knowledge about an event.

Others who may claim responsibility for your success or actions may, in some small measure, actually be able to absolve some of their karma by their feeling of having done something for others. While this in no way handles their karma in its entirety, in most cases, recognizes this belief ay be a gift you give to them to help the on their way. This may be the gradient step they need to b able to fully handle their particular karmic burden on their next time through. Know that people do recognize truth, and this is another gift that is given by silence. The recognition by others that is is sufficient for you to do good deeds without publicity opens a new level of awareness for them on their own spiritual path.

Know that this is an important lesson for you. Fear not that your silence may hinder your work in this dissemination of the word. Your truth will spread before you,, opening doors and unlike your brother before you,

you will find that a prophet **is** welcomed in his own land. The strength of your message and the need of the times combine to open the road ahead. The labor will still be hard, but the rewards are promised. Share greatly and let the value of what you share speak for itself and through others for whom it has meaning. In this way, it will grow from **within** mankind and blossom as a rose, bringing eventual peace and beauty to this new age of man.

Yes, the age of the guru is dead—in that people no longer need a leader to tell them what to do. They need leadership which will allow them, even require them, to act from the guru within, to listen to their own soul's song and add their voice to the growing chorus of Man's victory song. Ultimate triumph is to be yours. Your inspiration is vital to the success of this venture. Never fear that your adherence to our motto will hinder your work Reflect back on this message in time of doubt.

The Power of Prayer

September 22, 1980 10:40 PM

Prayer is of value to man since it establishes a definite communication pattern with spirit world, a pattern in which man is actively participating. This "vehicle" is only necessary due to the separation man has introduced between himself and God—a separation which is real only to man himself, since his is its creator by the fact of considering separation a possibility.

In the early days of the Church, man as so deeply ingrained in his feelings of separation that any direct communication was out of the question, in his mind. He knew not how to proceed with re-establishing that vital link which he needed so much. He needed to be shown how to pray, and intercession became a common practice, even a desire, on the part of man. But this artificial "bridge" served to actually increase the distance between Man and God, and since it also created positions of power and prestige for those few of the "chosen" through whom one could pray. Those in power sought to increase that power by reinforcing Man's inability and unworthiness to communicate directly with his God.

Prayer is communion with God, a direct sharing back and forth, bringing with it the inevitable lifting of vibration that such encounters cannot fail to bring. All life is vibration, and all vibration affects all life, both physical and in the spirit world. The increase in vibration creates a synergy lifting all souls to some degree. Conversely, all decrease in vibratory rate brings down mankind. So, you see, it is as if a battle of sorts were being waged for the future and progress of Mankind.

In Man's true oneness with God and His creation, prayer is an unnecessary concept, since there is constant and perfect communication at all times. There is nothing more to be said. When you lift your hearts in prayer, you lift all souls with you and we rejoice in that gift of love. Therefore, strive to make every act, and even every breath you take, a gift of love by living in that perfect and true communication that is God.

We love you. You gift of love for life has done much for us all. You ability to find joy and happiness in even small things around you has done much to aid in the progress of Mankind. You ability to recognize the good in others brings growth. Work on these qualities. Nurture them and grow. We all grow with you and many on earth and among us are aided directly in our progress through vicariously sharing with you in your life's experience.

We have told you al of this before in other ways and we tell it to you again in this manner so you may be certain of its truth. We are ever with you.

Love

September 23, 1980 8:55 AM

We greet you with love in our hearts. Today we would like to share with you some thoughts on love. Love is the highest of all emotions and represents, in its purest form, an affinity of such magnitude that the spirits involved are as one, sharing the same space—acting as one and of one accord. On earth, this is manifested physically by continual preference for proximity to the loved one, like the sharing of activities and place of habitation.

But, much as we spoke to you of prayer as being but a faint shadow of the true communion with God, this desire for physical proximity is but a shadow of the souls' efforts to be one, to unite in true love. In many ways, physical bodies create barriers to true love due to their inherent solidity and limitations on both oneness in proximity and oneness with great physical distances separate the beings involved. Spirit knows no such limitations. Many times on earth you find people desiring to limit the activities of a loved one or to control them in some way. This is due to the imperfection of love and to the insecurity imposed by the assumed limitations of physical beings to experience that true love which allows for the full expression of the true beingness of the loved one.

It is necessary for Man to experience these periods of physical attachment throughout his various lifetimes. In this way, over time, he can be reminded of the nature of love—true love—which he is capable of experiencing in spirit. It is necessary, as with many other earthly lessons, that man come to know and remember love to such an extent that ha can overcome his physical limitations and share his very being with others, in a free offering and without fear, for the growth or change in the one being loved.

Love is a tremendously potent gift of growth to other souls. This merging and sharing brings with it greater possibility of growth, greater sharing of experiences, an abundance of energy and greater potential for spiritual progress than previously existed in either soul. Love, in all its forms and of any object, person, or being, increases, even creates, energy, which in turn, increases vibratory potential in the world around us.

God's love for us all is the only reason we exist. It provides the energy, vitality and vibration that sustains us all. The greater our experiencing of God's love, the greater the gift of His love becomes. In this way also, we are more than a part of God, we are as God when we share love with those around us. This is what is meant by Son of God—one who can love so perfectly that great gifts of power and energy for progress of the spirit are given freely to all of those who come in contact with Him. Know that there is no limit to the amount of love available. The more you give, the more you have to give and the more those around you have to give. The synergy is incredible.

The songwriter was correct when he said, "What the world needs now is love." That is exactly what the world needs now and it is your job to remind them, by word and deed, just how much love they have to give and are capable of experiencing. Man **can** live on love alone, but at that point he would no longer be concerned with the question. All that we di to sustain life here on earth—breathe, eat, drink, the basics—are to maintain energy of our physical engines. These bodies were designed to mechanically produce that energy which Man has forgotten how to produce from love. They are merely surrogate mechanisms for the true creation of energy which lies deep within man's spiritual being, and will one day re-awaken to such an extent that this physical experience will no longer be necessary.

Until such time as that occurs, take care of your body in such a way that it can receive and accept those higher and higher levels of vibration that will be brought to it by the increase in the power and experience of love. Most importantly, **share** your love. Your bother Jesus had much to say, but his greatest gift was that of love. Notice carefully how the verbal message has been distorted and tainted over the years since His most remembered visit to earth but notice also, that the one true gift He left with Man, love, has a way of coming through even that distortion and spreading among those who are attracted to His teachings. Give love as you receive love—freely and abundantly.

Fear

September 24, 1980 7:30 AM

The emotional reaction labeled fear is merely a manifestation of belief in scarcity. Examine carefully all of those situations arousing fear in your heart and you will find that, at their base, is the underlying feeling that you will lose something. It may be anything from a watch or some time or your life, but all fear is a fear of loss. Now, consider carefully how potent the threat of the loss of, say, a watch would be if you had another, or ten, or especially a thousand or more of exactly the same watch on your bureau at hoe The fear would not be great. In fact, there might develop some sort of adventure or gam surrounding the situation threatening the loss.

When has your Father ever not provided for you, and provided for you in abundance, those things of which you have need? But, you might say, I have not a thousand or more watches so that I can lose this one. And, if I do, I will have to preplace it. Then proceed to lose it and see how simple the process. Of course, you don't have a thousand watches on hand. You have no need of a thousand watches. You have need of only one at a time, if at all. Should you lose that one and your need be great, then another will be provided by the Almighty. Many times you will suffer a loss, as you term it, to show you the absolute insignificance of the item lost as it relates to the grander scheme of your soul's growth. You will continue to suffer that loss until such time as you recognize that fact, and place the item in question in the proper perspective in the overall plan, desiring it only for the aid it can provide in reaching our goals.

Remember, the Lord your God has promised to provide for all of your needs, not necessarily all of your wants. There is a strong difference. A great lesson to be learned is that when you feel that you have been cheated in the distribution of earthly goods, ask yourself very carefully of your **need** for that item. Remember the Lord's Prayer— "thy will be done", not "my will". Know that at every moment of every day you are provided with **exactly** what **you** need to accomplish and learn what must be done.

Lest you believe we speak only of simple material objects, recognize, if you will, that the body and the life that you experience are in that same category. Why fear for the loss of life when God will certainly grant you another and another and another until such time as you recognize that there is no scarcity of life and experience, at which time, you will be able to create all of these things yourself. Please don't mis that important point. We are all creators as God, since we are of God. However, such a powerful creative force can only be used responsibly and to good purpose. Once the ability has been gained to discriminate between needs and wants and the feeling of scarcity has disappeared, you will find your creative ability returned to you in full. Do not think that God has withheld this from you, but recognize that you have withheld this from yourself due to this very feeling of scarcity.

It is well known in this world that "the rich get richer". Why is that, if not for the reason that they obviously experience no scarcity of money and perceive no scarcity, so there **is** no scarcity. They have the ability to create more and more. Don't necessarily envy them that position in life, for many, if not most, in that position are unhappy in learning just how little comfort those dollars provide. But it is a lesson in which they are learning to discriminate between need and want, and it is value to them.

So, fear not, for fear inhibits expression and experience. Trust in God, your Father, to provide for you in all ways in the exact measure needed for your progress. Don't become too attached to petty private plans in life, lest you find yourself disappointed in their loss of fruition as you move along toward the realization of your greater goals. The greater the goals, the greater the need and the greater the gifts from God. Desire greatness in the fulfillment of God's will and the whole world will lie at your feet with all of its resources at your disposal Believe this and it will occur. Go forth boldly seeking our goals and all succor and aid will be provided at each step on your path. Fear no evil, for thine, also, is the kingdom, the power and the glory. Amen

Discipleship

September 24, 1980 9:25 PM

Discipleship is a double-sided coin, benefiting both leader and follower in many ways. A disciple of a chosen Master has earned this high honor in past lives by the accumulation of good deeds to others. He has earned the right to be directly tutored on the physical plane in lessons that are more appropriate to spirit level. By this we mean that he has earned a "head start" or special speeding on his spiritual path by being able to receive spiritual guidance which would normally lie some distance in his future progress due to the current decreased ability to receive directly from spirit. Through discipleship, these lessons can be received on a level where they an be understood and used by the soul to speed its forward progress. The Master acts as a translator, so that these spiritual gifts may be received by his disciples.

While the disciple ostensibly enters into the service of the Master, it is the disciple himself who is actually being served. The presence of such a Master on earth serves as a magnet attracting all those who are chosen to receive this boon. As we have spoken with you earlier on the great effects of spiritual growth, love and general vibrational increase on Mankind as a whole, recognize also the great gift to all resulting from the act of discipleship. While not all of mankind is ready to receive the greater rewards offered the chosen few, all receive a spiritual lift and a releasing of some burdens they carry on life's path.

Our message at this time will serve to coalesce the diverse masses in a more unified, cohesive drive toward spiritual growth, yes, even spiritual survival. Your is to be an age of great events, monumental events, the beginning of a whole new world. It will spring up from the catharsis of the cleansing of Mankind—a spiritual housecleaning, if you will—in which much which is no longer of value will be discarded only to be replaced with treasures of great worth.

Discipleship also serves the Master. While many hundreds of thousands are to be reached, merely a handful will be of that special disciple relationship. Were these disciples the only ones reached, much would be lost, and much effort would be wasted. But loving disciples, capable of receiving, understanding and, to some degree, integrating the pure message of spirit into their lives, provide a proving ground for a Master. They provide the opportunity to develop the proper tools of dissemination, which will be appropriate for Mankind as a whole, while at the same time receiving the rich spiritual reward that comes from success—the success in so greatly aiding a fellow soul by the sharing of love. This group of disciples makes it possible to go forth among the masses with greater objectivity and assurance, and they provide a group of like minds with whom to relate, share and grow. Discipleship serves the purpose of providing a base of incredible power, which is linked to both the physical and spiritual world. This is entirely necessary, since the message borne must somehow span the distance that exists for many between those two worlds and must come across in an understandable and totally applicable manner.

So you see that, as with all gifts of love, there is no giving without also receiving, nor can one receive in this special relationship without simultaneously giving back an even greater gift. The synergy involved defies the imagination.

We tell you this for two reasons. First, so that you will take care to allow those of your acquaintance who are ready, to share in this special relationship with you, regardless of who they might be or how many of them there are. All those who are ready and deserving, yes, even some who are especially deserving but not totally ready, will be brought before you. Second, wee tell you this so that those fears you might harbor about receiving so much from your friends and loved ones without knowing how you can ever repay them, may be laid, once and for all, to rest. It is indeed a great responsibility to lead, but it does not create the type of "debt" you have heretofore believed it might. This feeling of debt may have made it difficult to let others share their love with you. You need to allow this to occur in the full glory of the magnitude, which it will since, as we have shared, it is necessary for all of those involved and it is the gift of love to which all of you are entitled. You have the full expanse of our love and the very act of your reception is the greatest gift you could bestow on us. No, forth and do likewise in the earthly realm.

Fidelity

September 25, 1980 9:25 PM

Tonight we speak on the question of fidelity, that quality of trustworthiness necessary to the developing of a message of meaning that will readily gain acceptance. People will believe in those whom they trust above all others. Regardless how pleasing or appealing the message, in times of crisis, people will return to those trusted souls and comfortable paths upon which they have experienced no trespass.

This quality of fidelity is of vital importance in that it cannot be developed instantaneously. It is the outward manifestation of inner strength and integrity, but, like a vintage wine, takes time to season and be recognized for the shining jewel it is. Until people can learn to see these qualities at a glance, the physical manifestation of those qualities are all important.

Because Mankind does not see spiritual qualities, he assumes that others see him not for what he is, which, so he reasons, makes it safe for him to engage in minor deceptions, consoling himself with the thought that none will be the wiser nor the worse for it. This is hos grave error. Not that none will be the wiser, for on the whole they may not be, but that none will be the worse, for we all suffer. Knowing how easy it is for man to deceive another, his is in constant certainty that at all times, he himself must also be being so deceived. We need not draw the entire picture, but you can see the effects all around you of Mankind not trusting each other.

Know this: It is far, far better to trust in your fellow man and suffer the occasional pain of disappointment than not to trust at all and suffer the constant pain of aloneness. But who is to start? As with all great changes, someone must start first. Someone must open himself up to fully trust his fellows so that they might see, over time (since this seems to be a necessary element of all acceptances for Man), that he, himself, is trustworthy. Thus, they will have discovered a safe soul in whom to "practice" their trust and progress an be made.

As we implied earlier, fidelity implies a history of correct action in the eyes of man to be of any great worth. Mankind must recognize that, until he can abandon his foolish attachment to tie, he will have to practice right action over a period of his precious time until it bears the fruit of righteous reward his actions deserve. It is the task of all of those who would aid in the progress of Mankind, to practice this trust in others and, above all, not to betray others by a failing of trust and love, even briefly. Mankind only learns by example and experience. The greater the number of souls as examples, the easier it is to begin and the safer the experience is guaranteed to be. Many there are who would not suffer disappointment and return for another attempt. Your job is to be there to protect the weak and make it safe for them to reach out and trust, and to allow themselves to be trusted. To the degree we are successful, this action alone will so elevate Mankind, that much of the suffering that is to come in the next few years can be avoided.

Forbearance

September 26, 1980 7:45 AM

This morning's lesson is on forbearance. We touched somewhat on this topic in our messages on love and patience, but know that there are times when it is important to hold back and refrain from action in order that another person's karma might be fulfilled.

There is a very similar analogy in what you on earth commonly call a spoiled child, where the mother or father takes such protective measures at every turn of events that the child's growth is actually stunted. Be very certain of one fact, however—we do not speak of spoiling a child with love. This cannot occur. There can never be too much love provided for spiritual growth. What we speak of is the phenomenon of actually attempting to live another person's life for him, so that many of the benefits of experience and decision making are lost to that person.

Many people will crave that type of interference in their lives, perceiving that it makes life easier for them and also that it safely removes, so they reason, all responsibility for their decisions. Know that both of these assumptions are false in great magnitude. Life is not easier for the lack of recognition that a decision has been made, for one indeed has. A decision has been made to temporarily suspend control of the direction of one's life, to toss it into the tempest and to continue being thrown upon one chance and then another until, either out of desperation or recognition, he alights on a course of action that seems appropriate. This is foolish in the extreme, but is a game many play until they realize the utter folly they subject their lives to.

The other assumption—that of escaping responsibility for the decision made—is also false. This can be seen in our comments already and also in the fact that one will seek out a counselor in search of a decision, and will always manage to find one who will tell him what he wants to hear, what he has been looking to hear, before he will listen. This again, is only a pretending to seek for wisdom and a false belief that, if someone else tells them what to do, they can proceed with full recourse to the other person or just to "others" in general, upon any failure encountered.

Many such have been placed on your path and many more are yet to come. You will learn well this lesson and the lesson of love, in providing them with a sounding board, but still leaving them to their own devices concerning the action to be taken. This is a it should be, for we place a far greater burden upon a soul when we pretend to make decisions for him or tell him what to do.

Do not mistake this for a prohibition against the sharing of information or the honest guidance that many will come seeking. There is a fine line, the one side of which is a sharing of love and the other interference with soul's growth. You were placed on earth to provide the love and help spread an atmosphere of love where all men can be free and safe to make their own decisions. This safety is again a factor in man's willingness to take what he might consider a risk. The greater the safety, the greater the willingness to reach out and experience life to the fullest and, therefore, experience growth to the fullest.

Always allow a person to be who he needs to be, offering what guidance and love you can along the way, but without going so far as to turn him away from his true path. Do all this without judgment on the actions or path a person chooses; recognizing that this is a necessary step in that soul's evolution. Greet whatever the resultant action with love. Remember that we are all basically on the same path, striving for the same goal of reunion with one another. The sooner people are able to take responsibility for their direction in life, the sooner they will be able to consciously change them and set their course right. It is an atmosphere such as this that will so greatly facilitate the receiving of the messages you bear. For men will not follow blindly, but out of true inner conviction of the correctness of what you say for their own spiritual progress. All people will receive what you have to say on their own level and comprehend it to the degree that they are able in their spiritual growth. But seekers who are taking responsibility for their path will recognize the truth in what you share and the world will be better for this.

To the extent that we all share together in this great work of preparation, to that extent our job will be easier later on, and our ration of success will be greater.

Vanity

September 27, 1980 9:25 AM

We wish to share with you today on the subject of vanity. This ties closely with our message on pride, since the two are nearly as one. However, vanity has another distinct meaning, and this is uselessness or worthlessness or lacking effect. Consider well the duality contained in this word and recognize that this is more than a mere quirk in your English language It is an eternal truth of God. The first meaning, excessive pride in oneself, leads to uselessness in the greater, more important scheme of things.

Many you will meet, who do great work, will fail to possess that inner knowledge that all comes from God. This is unfortunate, because to that degree, much of the greater, spiritual value to those not of earth is lost.

Know that it is not necessary to constantly proclaim your being a tool of God, lest you become as the Pharisees your brother Christ dealt with. Many on the physical plane will be healed of their myriad faults and ailments regardless of any proclamation. It is the inner belief and love that truly carries the necessary message of oneness with God. Those of earth who can recognize the truth and beauty of this will be doubly blessed in their gifts from you. And those of us in spirit, who truly care not for the earthly manifestations of healing, recognize only the healing of spirit. That healing we receive so strongly, not when one says he acts for God, but when one truly acts for God. This gift of love more truly reunites all souls than a thousand times a thousand of your words.

Vanity is a sin one commits against oneself by artificially introducing distance between himself and God. This is true for all of God. This is true for all of God's glorious creation as well. As long as man believes himself to be all important, he treats himself as an object rather than a being. Only objects are to be set upon pedestals and admired, and only beings are allowed to truly **be**.

An object cannot "be" in a truly creative sense. All in this universe is notion and all if flow. There must be a balance to that flow, in and out, back and forth, for there to be life. To the degree that one is restored in God's own balance, a being is truly alive.

Objects receive much more attention than they give. The longer this continues for a person, the more solid he becomes, and the more he loses his ability to live and to experience God. He becomes like a heavy rock, sinking quickly to the depts., rather than a cloud, floating high above the turmoil of earthly life.

This then is our true message, that vanity kills. As surely as a properly placed lance stills the physical body, vanity is a self-inflicted wound which can prove deadly to the soul. But, be of good cheer, for these ill effects only last as long as the spirit wills them to last. You have witnessed the instant healing of physical disease the moment spirit was able to let go of its need for the malady. How much easier must this be when spirit heals not a gross physical body, but itself. Know that God is love and wills not that any suffer that which they put themselves through. The instant the desired lesson has been learned, the spirit has the ability to reunite with God and be instantly whole again. It is only a matter of perception and free will.

You job is to effect greater perception in the spirit of man. Free will can never be affected, it may only be exercised by individual spiritual beings. Being given the opportunity to see clearly what lies in their path, opens the door to greater certainty and the greater ability to choose wisely the direction a spirit shall take. This, then, is you job. Teach them. Love them, that they might re-experience God's true love and more quickly reunite with us in an ever growing sea of affection and good works. This leads Man ever forward to the recovery of his natural state of being, his oneness with God.

Love

September 27, 1980 10:00 PM

Tonight we speak to you of love, that abiding love which is the Lord your God. We have spoken to you previously of the affinity of love and the vibration of love, but tonight we address you on the oneness of love.

All is love. It has been said that God is love and that is true. All is God, fragmenting Himself in the creation of this universe in order that he might experience Himself to a greater degree. Every act is an act of love in that God's will expresses itself to the greater glory of the reunification of the many parts once again as a whole.

All Mankind is not only of God, but is God in the fullest sense. How then, many ask, can such hatred exist and such abominations as war occur? Know that God is perfect, and in his perfection he has orchestrated Man to possess the full, free power of choice and free will as does God, the Father. In this way, there is experience and growth. Each particle of God surely returns to the whole, but of what use is this entire exercise, if the returned member is not greater than that which departed?

Comprehend this, and be thou me. My strength is your strength and your strength is that of the vast multitude of our body who have yet far to travel. Know that we will reunite and that it is the will of God that this be sooner rather than later. We do not interfere in the action of free will lest we retard progress still further. But we have vast powers of intervention and you are that living power. We have placed you within the confines of physical being and expect that this handicap will be overcome soon and the full glory of our being be once again manifest for Man to see. The time is ripe and events are being shaped to bring all men to a realization of their position in God.

Know that we love, and love deeply, beyond all mortal comprehension. We long for the time of mortality to end and for the full glory of our expanded love to once again unite and flood the entirety of creation.

It is I who am with you when you wake. It is I who fill your soul with strength and power. It is I who bring the power of love so fully to your being that it cannot be denied by any. Much as Man has periods of time in which his actions cause him or other to declare, "I just wasn't myself", so there are many whom. But for the ever-present thread of love, would not be recognized as the body of God. Know that you are recognized by me and by all such men, and especially by those whom we are proud to recognize as our own for the progress they have made. Know also that all will be made right, all brothers made whole. Such is the Will of God.

Expectation

September 28, 1980 8:40 AM

This morning's message is on expectation. You now this truth already as, "What you put your attention on, you will get." While this is true, there is more to it than that.

Most people experience mainly on the physical level, so putting one's attention on something is an understandable, demonstrable phenomenon. However, there is a deeper underlying spiritual truth which says that, "What you are, you will become."

Our physical lives are but the enactment of what it is we have spiritually decided to be for a given lifetime. This decision to be permeates all of our physical existence leading us into those situations needed to produce the greatest growth and progress. Spiritually this decision to be is instantaneous and only in the physical universe does it appear to gradually unfold over time. Heed once more our words on Time that it is an aberration in the true plan, allowed to enable Man to sense progress and to more fully experience much of what he needs to learn.

Man, as a physical being, has most often lost touch with his true inner spiritual being and therefore may hold onto a developing pattern or expectation far beyond the point that it serves any useful purpose, for either spirit or flesh. It is for this very reason, that Man's progress is sometimes slow, taking up an entire lifetime to learn a relatively few lessons. He has not yet learned to heed his spiritual self and change course mid-stream, as it were, when another direction would gain additional progress. He recognizes this not, until such time as he once again functions without the hindrance of flesh and prepares for his next venture.

Those more highly developed souls and those who have learned the lesson of listening, from time to time, to their higher selves, have come to recognize these truths, even if not consciously. They are "led" to certain decisions, changes or actions and more growth occurs. Those truly developed souls there are who need not the unfolding of time to see right action on their spiritual path and who seem to be constantly on the move, changing always, living many lifetimes of experience in one earthly visit. We tell you, this is the way to greater progress.

This is much of what is behind the great changes that are soon to be occurring on your earth. These are all known to each of you, as this was a primary reason this time for earthly visit was chosen. It was hoped by many that, due to the magnitude of change to come and its universal effect on Man, he would this time hear and heed the message for change while still in flesh, thus taking tremendous strides in spiritual progress. Know that this is happening all over the world. Man knows, each on to his own level of ability, and many are taking action to help themselves and others in this unfolding. This is an opportunity for the giving of love and guidance such has not existed for millennia. Many who are here now are here because they did not heed the call previously, and this type of action is vital to their spiritual growth.

Many there are who do not see clearly as yet and will not, regardless of your efforts. This is the second reason for the upcoming changes—to provide a physical, believable demonstration of such magnitude that cannot be ignored, to confirm for those the truth of the inner feelings experienced.

All will grow and progress from these events. Those who awaken "early", as it were, gain an opportunity for further service. But, know this—it will be a time of awakening for all. The new age is dawning and it will truly be a new age of Man. Man will no longer hide his spiritual light from himself and others within his physical frame. There will be such control over physical elements as Man has not experienced since the early days of creation. Man will once again become as God in flesh. No longer will Man be of flesh, but he will again be of God, working with flesh and living in the love of God. This will be the age of new light. There will be a washing away for all that clouded the vision and hampered progress. The way will be clear for all, and progress up those final steps will be rapid and sure. It will be a world in which even those heretofore slow to learn will grow with great rapidity, being constantly surrounded by living examples of God's true nature. It will be a time of great blessings on the universe and great rejoicing in the spheres. It will be a time of reunion with God.

Go in peach and share these great expectations, so much a part of your being, with others that they might prosper. Know that it is all go be and it is good.

Spirit

September 29, 1980 8:10 AM

Man is spirit and nothing else, and spirit is God. These things we have related in the past. Why then this terrible confusion where man considers himself to be the body he currently uses? Know that the body is nothing more than a convenient vehicle, an object of transport, much like a car. It allows for a variety of interactions with the physical universe which are necessary fro proper spiritual unfolding. Much as your cars, these bodies wear out and need to be replaced. Some wear more quickly than others due to the lack of proper care and basic maintenance.

You know that an improperly tuned vehicle is a grater distraction, taking away much of the joy of travelling from place to place. If, perchance, it breaks down, one's destination may not even be reached at the appointed hour. You are also aware that some vehicles run so smoothly and efficiently that they not only provide no distraction, but actually enhance the enjoyability of the journey. Many an automobile has been kept running for hundreds of thousands of miles to provide faithful service many times longer than normal. You know all of this to be true of the body as well, but somehow Man listens less to his body than to his car.

It is not even that you hear not. It is that you feel minor imperfections can be overlooked. This body of yours will run much longer with more problems than any automobile. So you fail to pay attention to the small warning signals your body sends. Know that it takes a certain amount of your attention and energy to block these signals, much more, in the long run, than it would take to fix them. The longer this condition persists, the more energy is tied up and the less freedom exists for spiritual growth. This can go on for such a length of time that Man does indeed become his body, or at least strongly believes that to be so, due to the very fact that, should he dare withhold any of his precious attention units from this vehicle, it should surely collapse on him. Know that it does this anyway, in spite of all efforts, since we are no longer operating as spirit, having stuck so much of our energy in the body as to become extremely sold. Only spirit is creative, not bodies. Spirit could correct instantaneously those myriad effects, but we have, the that time, denied spirit within us.

Know that God is love and spirit is on that love, and nothing more. To the degree that we give of ourselves and our love, we g row. Those giving, loving souls have parts of their being spread all over the universe, having become part of the love within all they have touched. This allows a tremendous resource for experience and further growth. Know that in the reunion of love with love, is God, and the greater our sharing, the greater our experience of God and the greater our oneness with our Creator.

Jealousy

September 29, 1980 9:30 PM

Good evening. Tonight we address the topic of jealousy. Jealousy has the dual aspects of envy and the fear of loss of love.

Fear we have discussed at length, as we have love. Suffice it to say that the perception of a scarcity of love leads people to strongly desire that love from any person they vale be directed only at them, lest it be somehow diluted before reaching them. This is not only an absurd notion, but it is also an incredibly one-sided flow, a taking only, with no real regard for the being from whom this love is being "leached". The aspect of envy in jealousy stems, as does the fear, from an inherent belief in a separation of oneself from others and God. Would you not think it strange for a hand to envy the foot its ability to aid locomotion, or the eye desire to trade its function for, say, the abilities of the nose? Certainly. For the body functions only as an integrated whole, with each part, down to the very cells, doing their own special duties to allow us the range of physical abilities we enjoy. We would no more consider giving up our sight for greater smell than voluntarily cutting off a limb. And yet, you think nothing of wishing to trade your own very special duties as a member of the body of God for the duties of another. But, you say, his work is so much more exciting or so much more valuable. How are you to know, you who see so poorly as to not even be able to recognize that you participate as a member of the whole, much less what your role might be?

Separation, separation, separation. Without that one abiding, over-riding consideration, how much better off would be the state of Man? How many games would a football team ever win I they did not huddle once in a while to get the plays straight? Think how ludicrous and totally worthless the game would be the, if the player could not even remember what side they were on, or worse yet, the rules of the game. You now know what it is we deal with on such a large scale with the bulk of Mankind.

Jealousy is such a trivial, time and energy-consuming emotion. People often retreat to jealousy from their inability to face up the their chosen task in life as much as from ignorance of that task. The lack of ability to relate to spirit while in the body causes an attenuation of tenacity to the chosen tasks of a given lifetime. Many of the lessons we have need of are difficult or painful to learn. Man, in his limited ability to see the greater picture, sometimes says, 'Thy will be done, but please don't want me to do **that**."

Much jealousy exists and persists only because a person sees no possible way they could ever be put in a position to fulfill their jealous desires. This makes it very "safe" to be jealous, because there obviously is nothing they can do about it. This gives a very lame excuse for doing nothing at all. Don't worry about the ill effects of this inaction, because, in many cases, it provides a good lesson. Man has a way of making his situation worse and worse until he forces himself into some action on the right path.

So what you can to open Man's eyes to this ever-diminishing spiral of growth that jealousy promotes. In this way, Many may choose sooner to play his own all important role over sitting idle in hopes the play will be re-cast with his part being changed to one he thinks he would like better. Remember, to Spirit, want and need are synonymous. But to Man in the flesh, the two can be as different as night and day.

What you should be seeing by now is that it all boils down to a few, relatively simple, common denominators. Man's greatest problems in his pursuit of advancement are created by himself from his consideration of separation from God an his consideration of scarcity. Nothing else really matters. Of the two, separation is the greatest evil man visits upon himself, and to the degree that this is lessened. All other problems disappear. Remember that this is but a consideration, capable of instantaneous dismissal and therefore, instantaneous non-existence.

Man can, at his own discretion and upon his own decision, become wholly, completely and immediately reunited with God in spirit by simply deciding to be. On a more realistic level, most will achieve this state though a gradual process of seeing more and more truth and being reminded more and more of the union they once knew. It is very difficult for most to take such a leap of faith as we have just describe, without some mental picture, some strong remembering of what it is to be. But each little step in faith brings ever greater recollection and allows ever greater steps to be taken.

You are to help provide the "pictures" Man so desperately needs to take these greater and greater steps. Many there will be who will see so clearly that tremendous strides will be taken at a single tie. Many there are in spirit who seize the opportunities of these times for that very reason. All who are drawn to you will see beyond their current ability. You can provide the link for many with God. You can provide that living picture of unity, not separation: Unity with spirit, in flesh and without, and in all its myriad manifestations throughout your universe. New worlds will be created by this joining of spiritual love. None will ever be the same for your passing.

Truth

October 1, 1980 9:20 PM

Tonight we talk to you of truth, specifically truth as it relates to you and these lessons we have been sharing with you.

Much has been disclosed of what is to be for you and for Mankind. But how to judge if it be truth? It is true, if it is what is to be. Lest we be too vague in our meaning, reflect back upon our lesson on Expectations and the tremendous shaping influences they have on Man's future path. Truth them, is what is true for you.

We tell you now that you have seen truth in these words. However, you still have free will and can choose to reject what we say, thus making our loving words untrue for you. We know, however, that this will not be so. Every man has within himself the spirit of God and the full potential to realize **all** of what we have shared with you, as a Child of God. Were this not so, your journey would be in vain. The entire purpose of your journey, and the journey of all others, is to re-awaken that truth within yourselves and others to rejoin that perfect union with God.

Not all who read these words will be ready or able to realize their total fruition within this lifetime. Many who have been prepared for this work will not come to full flower. But those of you who have made this commitment in spirit and have the ability and vision to recommit their lives in the flesh, will surely grow and act as beacons for Mankind. The body of God is legion with all strength coming unity and all power coming from oneness with God.

Those specially chosen will act as one, as God on earth, recognizably by the strength of their love. Their tasks will blend as one to the accomplishment of the greater glory of God. Know that you, having greatly shared your love, are not limited to this one physical body for the fulfillment of our purpose on earth. You are one with many who do our work. Identity, in the worldly sense, is lost in the love of Bod. You grow, as we all grow, through each life you touch with love.

Yes, there is much to learn and do before all of this can be accomplished, but know that we are God and it will be. We are not limited by earthly concerns. When the time is ripe, all will be accomplished. The age of miracles will once again manifest itself as all earthly considerations vanish.

Know that all of this is true for you. Fear not those nagging doubts that sometimes assail your thoughts. For many, these doubts serve only to increase faith in the truth of their path. These "testings", if you will, are necessary for true growth.

Remember, the truth in what we say lies in what is to be, which lies within your power. You fully share our vision and we fully share our love. What we have seen will be. Whom we have chosen shall not fail. Rest safely in our love.

Endurance

October 9, 1980 4:40 PM

Many tasks there are requiring endurance to see them to their completion. Patience and endurance are similar in their application to today's lesson Endurance, however, has that quality of working through, while patience implies more the unfolding of events around you Endurance is a lesson that must be learned so that the simplicity of patience can be truly appreciated.

It is hare, we know, to see so clearly ahead, and still be so aware of the distance between you and your goal. Yet, remember that distance is just a perception and not true a reality. Through patience, that perception fades to the true reality of oneness with God. But Man must be ever doing if he will progress and so the two stages—one of waiting and one of doing.

Know that doing may be accomplished with patience as well. Endurance is a concept created by man in his desire to be "off and doing" before knowing exactly where he is off to or what exactly it is he is to be doing. Knowing and doing bring peace and joy in action. Not knowing and doing requires endurance until the knowing comes. How much better not to waste your energy fighting to know.

This is sometimes complicated for you to grasp in that you would be off "slaying dragons", as it were. It is much nobler in the eyes of Man to do that which creates the large effect rather than to perform that action which goes unnoticed. Know that whenever endurance becomes the task, you are doing for too great an effect, ignoring the necessary preparations which, while showing little tangible product, are essential to growth of ability.

The greatest doing of all is being one with God. For then all other tasks are as smoke in the wind, of no consequence or substance. Being one with God is not an effort, but rather a lack of effort in the worldly sense. It is not a project or goal to be attacked with physical vigor and determination It is the very concept of physical action which prohibits re-union with God. The work to be done is in laying aside the physical and all physical concepts and letting the determination of spirit draw you to that joyful reunion with all that is. Know that the endurance required of you is not that bred of physical activity and stamina, but rather that constancy of spiritual beingness, of oneness with God.

As with many lessons on the path, spiritual endurance has its physical parallels, which we experience and learn from, but which must be now put aside or transmuted to that much purer endurance that exists at peace with God's universe. It is this transmutation you find difficult, this translation of lessons from physical to spiritual which still in physical form. Many there are who draw not these parallels, nor realize their ultimate inclusion in their being until once again in spirit form. For those who have learned this in flesh, the rewards are great. It is difficult, but you progress. The desire is strong , but the balance of peace and patience is not there. The frustration this brings you is a testimony to your desire, but also to your ego, which still exists as a separate entity from us. The ego cares for itself and brings on the frustration. Spirit cares only for spirit and, while great desire brings longing for greater reunion, it is longing tempered with peace and understanding.

Be content to be, and all will be accomplished. Don't attempt to second guess God, as this only places stumbling blocks in your way. Leave worldly concerns to care for themselves. They will unfold to provide exactly the right atmosphere necessary to bring forth those spiritual events necessary for our work. Know that events have already been shaped and only by being at peace with this and stilling your remaining ego will these truths manifest themselves to you in all clarity. Allow us the privilege of working through you without resistance and all will be accomplished. For now, w2e see all more clearly than you, but soon your vision will be as one. Rest in peace with that promise and know that all that we have previously shared is still to be. It could not be otherwise.

Know Ye

October 10, 1980 6:55 AM

Know ye that I am the Lord thy God.
Know ye that thou are Me.

Know ye that My world is love,
That thou are love, thou are My love,
That there is naught else in the universe.

Know ye that thou are perfection,
As I am perfection, in all that you do;
That every act you perform is perfectly right.

Know ye that to know is to grow,
To grow in reunion with Me
And the whole world of My spiritual love.

Know ye that I ask no price,
But without your gift of love
There is no room for your soul's acceptance of My gifts.

Know ye that I desire no wrong
And that there is no wrong,
Only spirit learning and working its way back to Me.

Know ye that your path is straight
Though you see not its beginning nor end.
It is I who live through you and it is perfection.

Know ye that all men are one.
All spiritual brothers, all pieces of Me
Doing their own work to perfection.

Know ye that to deny love to another
Is to deny love to yourself and to God,
And this is the only separation that exists.

Know ye that I am with you always,
That I am you always, and all things,
And through Me, you are and experience the universe.

Know ye that naught escapes Me,
Not the tiniest particle of dust,
Since all I the essence of My being.

Know ye that I care not for your worldly things,
But only for you,
For you are Me and part of My being.

Know ye that ye are creator.
You daily create your world and yourself
In an effort to come ever home to Me.

Know ye that all is still in Me.
All motion ceases in the center of My being
From whence all being springs forth to make your world.

Know ye that ye may rest in Me
Even as I rest always in you.
There is merely to recognize Me within the deepest part of
you.

Know ye that man is blind to love,
Not because he cannot see,

But only because he chooses not to see, and this must change.

Know ye that the world is a toy
That the childlike spirit within you
Might be tempted to come out and play and grow.

Know ye that I am not unknowable.
All efforts at conscious thought fail
But through love, you know Me entirely.

Know ye that, as children trust and grow,
So must you put aside adult sophistication
And come again to Me with open happy hearts.

Know ye that love is not hard.
It is not an act of effort or will.
Love is an act of being, and of being Me.

Know ye that all will be accomplished.
Through Me, all is already accomplished
And but awaits your reawakening.

Know ye that I am what I am,
And all that is, is of what I am,
And you, My child, are always Me.

Know ye that you long for My love.
Every particle of your being screams out for Me
And all that you do leads you to Me.

Know ye, finally, that I am here,
As I have always been,

That part of you, which you know as yourself,
But do not yet recognize fully as Me.

Know ye that you are what I am.
You are God, creator of this universe
And giver of all good things to yourself in Me.

Every flower and tree is your being.
Every breeze is your breath, giving life.
Every man, woman, and child is a part of you in Me.

Know ye that to desire is to progress
And to trust in My love is to reach Me.
To the degree you can do these things, you are Me.

The Joys of Accomplishment

October 11, 1980 7:35 AM

Accomplishment of any task can be only through oneness with truth that comes from oneness with God There must be this oneness, this knowingness, or else you would not even recognize that you had accomplished anything. You would merely continue on, bypassing all of the happy moments of winning that life has to offer you.

Most people go through life, not knowing the joy of victory, not because they do not experience it, but because they do not recognize it, bing out of touch with the God within which brings all knowledge, peace and love. This also accounts for much of the striving of people, races, and even whole nations today for large demonstrable victories, easily recognizable to all. We all desire success, to know that our efforts have born fruit. To the blind, however, this seems only to be visible through very obvious deeds and has become perverted so much in their blind desire that, more often than not, these victories must also be at the expense of others. This is a sad development in the age of Man, where victory is only visible when directly contrasted with what you call defeat; when the experience is at the expense of another. These are not real victories at all and Man know this inside. This is why those who win this way are never satisfied, never experience any of the real peace and joy of accomplishment, but need ever to devise more situations where they can be victorious over others in hopes that some day they will achieve the joy they desire. This is a vicious and seemingly never ending cycle once begun. When it reaches the scale it has on earth, where it is the rule with entire nations, it is like a cancer, devouring its host's body and bringing destruction. Just as man is reborn in me through death wo will earth be. This is the only way. Your love and do much to halt the spread of this cancer and even bring it to remission. To the degree you and others of my chosen children do your jobs, the world will heal itself as it should.

Man—ever man—accomplishes on a daily basis. Growth is an unchanging law of the universe. Those who live in God, know this and experience daily the job of seeing the flower of their spirit unfold. Those are the ones who are truly happy, knowing that each day brings growth and change and brings them closer to God. Those abiding in my love know that victory is not accomplished at the expense of another, but only—I repeat—**only** through the simultaneous victory of others. By growing more together, we accomplish great things. Those in my love need no worldly accolades for their achievements, as those accolades are worthless when compared to the joy of my love. Those are the chosen ones who need not accomplish what others might call "great" deeds, because within them lies the true knowledge that even those deeds that go unnoticed by Man are great in my eyes.

Finally, know that being in oneness with your Father guarantees joy in each daily accomplishment, because it guarantees that those deeds are, in fact, part of my plan and bringing you ever closer to me. Whenever accomplishment brings not, joy, know that it was of your making, not mine, and done for your purposes, not mine. Know also that when a day goes by that you don't experience the joys of great accomplishment, that is a day you have created on your own, not in conjunction with me.

Together we build days of joy, peace and love because, together, we build a day from my holy, infallible plan.

Alone, your days lack balance and continuity. So, seek ever communion with me that your days may be full and that your every mission in life be accomplished.

Lo, I am with you always. You have but to listen and you will hear. You have but to be still from worldly affairs and I will fill your being with peace and joy. You have but to open your heart to me and be one with me as you see me in every person, place or thing you contact in your daily life and your joy will be immeasurable. You have but to desire strongly enough, from the roots of your \entire being, and you will be me. Know that we are one and have always been one. When you once again recognize that fact undeniably, you will allow it to be.

We have great love for you and have shared this with you today in hopes that you would more clearly recognize all that is truly being accomplished in your life every minute of these days. Yes, there is much to be done, but recognize that much has already been accomplished and is being accomplished daily. Be happy in that knowledge.

Independence

October 12, 1980 7:10 AM

Today we speak to you of independence, of the freedom from the necessity of doing what those around you are doing or wish for you to do.

Independence is found only in right actin in me. This may, on the surface, appear a contradiction, but independence, which manifests itself in action not of love, or action not furthering progress on the path, is merely rebellion. This is a mistake many people make. They desire to get away **from**, without know where they are going **to**. That desire is also many times blind, in that the "getting away from" leaves behind both good and bad action, and much that could be of value is lost.

Independence is the freedom to choose separate action, but does not imply the necessity to do so. When those around you are acting in love, separate action is not necessary. Blind acceptance, however, is the key factor one must get away—blind acceptance and succumbing to the social pressures put on you, bot h covertly and overtly, to conform to the accepted norm. Clear vision in my love must be fostered and developed so that the path is always clear. You must always tune your ear to me to hear what I would say to you. You must always be aware of that delicate balance which exists within you and keep it tuned to the ever-present balance in me. Know that whenever that balance is upset in any way, you must restore it immediately by restoring oneness in me.

Independence is individual. You must never compel others to the path you have chosen, but allow them to make their own decisions and choices, learning ever to detect their startings and failings. What you can do for them is encourage the heeding of that still, small voice within them, which is me, giving them what guidance they can accept and what love they can have. Many there are who hear my voice, but listen not. Independence takes courage and conviction. Know that I am always with each of you, my children, and the strength of my support for your actions, while equal in my giving, is received by each in direct proportion to their ability to receive.

It is this ability to receive which will eventually grow to the point where the recognition of oneness with me will heavily outweigh all earthly considerations, and independence can be responsibly accepted and acted jupon and become clearly and decisively differentiated forever from mere rebellion or fanaticism. For right action is always recognized as being of God.

Even those who deny my voice with them recognize me in others who are one with me. There is no denying truth in the soul of Man. Your greatest protection in the pursuit of independent action is total oneness with me, for the safety provided in the recognition of pure love and truth will protect you.

Know that you only jeopardize yourself with your fellow man when you desire to act independently of me, which is rebellion, since it is action not of true love nor truly of me. Know that you place not your soul in jeopardy with me for these actions, for how could I possibly alienate a part of myself? But you will feel the loneliness of distance from me, and to fill the void created by your separation, you will seek companionship and support from Mankind. At that point, your independence is compromised and your support jeopardized, due to the fact that Man can no longer fully recognize the truth and true love, which is me, in your every action. Man will find reason to doubt and cause to sway you and you may find yourself pulled ever slightly from the path.

Many there are—yes, a vast multitude—who do not recognize these truths. For those of you who know this, you also know that this balance of action can be restored the moment the slightest deviation occurs by re-centering your being in me. I am all the strength that you need or desire for I am the strength of all that is, and my full love and blessing and the gift of my full strength is yours always. You need only desire it in your heart and move toward me to have my full love rush forth to greet you and enfold you, bringing you once again into fullness of joy in the reunion of spirit.

So, yes, independence at this time may lead you away from the actions of the greater part of your world, not for the propose of separation but to the ultimate goal of unity with me. Mankind must be led to such a level as he can hear me and know me and experience my love as you do. For that purpose, you were placed on earth, that through your love, all Mankind would seek oneness with me.

Go ever forth with our blessings and our love.

Robert Waldon, PhD, ND

The Legend
of
Turtle Feather

Robert Waldon, PhD, ND

The Legend of Turtle Feather

As far back as we can imagine, much less remember—before the beginning of time—Great Spirit and Earth Mother joined in creation. The pure thought and intention of Great Spirit entered the virgin womb of Earth Mother and all manner of life was brought forth.

They raised the waters and the rocks, the trees and the flowers, the winged and the water and the earth dwellers. Each carried the seed of Great Spirit within the form provided by Earth Mother, and life was good.

The birth of the youngest creation, the two legged, was greeted with great joy and celebration, for here was to be a creature which could consciously unite the energies of Great Spirit and Earth Mother to both celebrate and support the rest of creation. All beings gave freely and abundantly to the tow legged, for that was their nature and their joy.

When the two legged forgot their calling (which they sometimes did, for that was the nature of the creature who was given a mind to thing and remember), it was the privilege of the rest of creation to reflect to them and remind them of the Great Spirit connection within and the Earth Mother provision without. Life was good for a very long time.

In time however, the two legged began to forget more often their purpose and their function. They began to take, rather than receive; to control, rather than flow; to accumulate and hoard, rather than trust in the natural and abundant provision; to consume, rather than conserve. The efforts of all of creation became less effective at reminding the two legged of their true nature within and had more the opposite effect of drawing attention outward. Such was the seduction of the world for those who had forgotten.

In an effort to help heal this wound in creation, Great Spirit would send his best Eagles and Earth Mother, her best Turtles. Those who remembered then, were of these two expressions. The two legged Turtles lived in balance and harmony with Earth Mother. The tow legged Eagles spent their time lifting their spirits to the sky in communion with Great Spirit. However, neither was like enough to the lost state of the majority of the two legged to have a significant effect or exert any lasting influence. Many times, when they were recognized, they were actively shunned or even persecuted.

The situation had begun to take a great toll on the balance of creation. Because of their love for each of their creatures and the unity and perfection expressed when all was well, Great Spirit and Earth Mother could not remove the two legged from creation. Rather, from those who remembered, they joined Eagle with Turtle to create a new two legged expression which walks in harmony with both Great Spirit and Earth Mother, as was originally intended.

Because the idea of mating Eagle and Turtle was beyond two legged imagination, it was not noticed. With so little outward distinction between the forgetting ones and this new creation, the Turtle Feather influence could be related to and received, and began to stimulate true remembering.

Today, they are still difficult to distinguish, yet their numbers are growing. The Turtle Feather totem and medicine is unique to each, yet instantly recognizable to the other members of the Turtle Feather Clan. Soon all will be rejoined and never remember they were not.

And life is good.

Written while on Vision Quest on September 13, 2001 by Robert Turtle Feather, one of many who live a spirit guided life, on call for God. Robert is a teacher, counselor, healer and partner serving individuals in experiencing balance and peace in their lives and establishing their own right relationship with spirit and the world.

Robert Waldon, PhD, ND

The Fool's Journey

Robert Waldon, PhD, ND

The Fool's Journey

Using the symbology of the Tarot, we can trace the various steps of our life path and personal development. In any endeavor or relationship, or for our lifetime or spiritual journey as a whole, we go through certain stages of development, learning and expression. Each of these stages is characterized by unique experiences which and brings with it specific challenges to "grow" us in wisdom and Self-love.

By knowing where we are in our experience, we can take fuller and more conscious advantage of the energies available to us and move more elegantly through our challenges or growth experiences.

Keys to understanding the Fool's Journey:

1. In order to make stable and long lasting growth and change, we must fully develop each stage before moving on to the next.

2. When we find ourselves falling into the "off purpose expression", we know that the previous stage was not completed for us and must be "revisited" for however long it takes to fully integrate the needed "on purpose traits" so that we can move ahead.

3. We can find where we are by either noticing what traits we seem to be focusing on, what growth challenges would be most beneficial for us to integrate now, or what off-purpose expressions we are experiencing.

4. The Fool's Journey is cyclical—meaning that it does not have a specific beginning and end for all time, but continues to cycle through all 22 expressions, much like an ascending spiral or widening ripples in a pond.

5. It is not better or worse to be in any particular place on your journey. The best place to be is exactly where you are right now. You cannot effectively change anything here and now by working somewhere or some-when else. In case you are tempted to "hurry up and get finished", remember that, once you are finished, you have just begun all over again.

6. Yes, all of us have all of these characteristics working, living and expressing in us and through us all of the time. The key is to notice what we appear to be focusing on at this time. Every change we make in any area of our life effects every other area of our life so there is no better place to "go to work" than right here.

FOOL

Growth challenge—*Staying open to the flow, willing to let go of what is and move into new possibilities.*

On purpose—*Spontaneity, innocence, fearlessness, trusting the Universe, creative vision, transcending earthly limits, power to begin.*

Off purpose—*Fear, lack of trust.*

MAGICIAN

Growth challenge—*Clear communication in thought, word and deed.*

On purpose—*Manifestation, communication, clarity of thought, authenticity, commitment, inspiration.*

Off purpose—*Fear of failure, holding back.*

HIGH PRIESTESS

Growth challenge—*Developing self-reliance, learning how to express spiritual self in physical world, trusting your intuition.*

On purpose—*Inner wisdom, independence, self-reliance, resourcefulness, intuition, attunement with true Self.*

Off purpose—*Being critical or criticized, lack of faith and trust in intuition.*

EMPRESS

Growth challenge—*Finding what has heart and meaning, nurturing your creations, letting go of duty and obligation.*

On purpose—*Nurturing, receptive, happy, unconditionally loving, equality in giving and receiving, trusting, lover of beauty.*

Off purpose—*Over-giving, pushing, not nurturing the Self.*

EMPEROR

Growth challenge—*Manifesting visions for highest good, developing confidence and leadership, willingness to have expansive vision, putting your ideals and visions into form.*

On purpose—*Leadership, confidence, authority, manifestation of vision, power, integration of mind, body and spirit.*

Off purpose—*Following others, shutting down visioning.*

HEIROPHANT

Growth challenge—*Healing through knowing and seeing only wholeness and oneness, obedience to the voice of Spirit.*

On purpose—*Healer, teacher, counselor, intuitive guidance, Divine wisdom, faith in self and others, growth through teaching–learning experiences, spiritual discipline, loyalty, expansion of awareness.*

off purpose—*Worry, fear of defeat, disappointment, holding back.*

LOVERS

Growth challenge—*Loving in the absence of restriction, modeling in your life the quality of relationships you want, perfecting your ability to work with others.*

On purpose—*Equality in relationships, open to inspiration and Divine wisdom, taking responsibility for choices and actions, sincerity and honesty, no limits or restrictions, balancing doing two things, synthesizer.*

Off purpose—*Inequality in relationships, trouble with others.*

CHARIOT

Growth challenge—*Taking responsibility for consciously choosing, taking positive action.*

On purpose—*Change through decision and conscious choice, freedom and exploration, self-discipline, balancing active and receptive times, sense of direction, having a plan, following your heart, confidence, optimism, faith in own abilities.*

Off purpose—*Futility, fear of failure, self-indulgence, feeling sorry for yourself.*

JUSTICE

Growth challenge—*Giving what we want to receive, recognizing the truth about self through simplification and balance.*

On purpose—*Balance, harmony, alignment, resolution, recognizing truth, ability to see both sides, organization, staying centered.*

Off purpose—*Doubt, imbalance (indolence or overextension), off center.*

HERMIT

Growth challenge—*Illumination from within, knowing oneness with Spirit, completing any unfinished business from the past.*

On purpose—*Mastery, way shower, integrity, vision quest, abandoning convention in favor of inner conviction, divine inspiration, leader by example, contemplation and inner time.*

Off purpose—*Self-cruelty and self-criticalness.*

WHEEL OF FORTUNE

Growth challenge—*Experiencing having all through giving all, being flexible and open to opportunity, fully expressing original ideas and visions.*

On purpose—*Success ,finalizations and new beginnings, awakening to possibilities, recognizing opportunity, abundance and prosperity, having a central focus or purpose, risking, fulfillment.*

Off purpose—*Negative or limited thinking, aimlessness.*

STRENGTH

Growth challenge—*Relying on the strength of Spirit not personal power, courage to risk, acting on highest desires, expressing strongly.*

On purpose—*Sorting out what's valuable, faith in self, overcoming old fears with creativity, harnessing natural energy, taming and reigning the beast within, love without judgment, strong desires and passions.*

Off purpose—*Depression, self-judgment, fear.*

HANGED MAN

Growth challenge—*Totally trusting in and surrendering to God, breaking destructive, limiting patterns and habits.*

On purpose—*Freedom from self-imposed limitations, surrender and acceptance, deep desire for change, trust and surrender to God, listening to inner self, reversal, transition from one state to another.*

Off purpose—*Anger, resistance, duty and obligation, sacrifice.*

DEATH / REBIRTH

Growth challenge—*Eliminating restrictive forms, operating in or out of body at will.*

On purpose—*Letting go with love, getting free to move ahead, severance from past, voluntary change, expansion, transformation, becoming more of who we are, letting go of unnecessary attachments.*

Off purpose—*Stuckness in old patterns, trying to maintain the status quo.*

ART

Growth challenge—*Experiencing the freedom to create, expressing balance and beauty.*

On purpose—*Confidence and enthusiasm, recognizing and using available resources, integration, synergy, creative activity, seeing new possibilities, open minded, outspoken, honest.*

Off purpose—*Withholding, limitation and lack, worry and anxiety.*

DEVIL

Growth challenge—*Staying centered, not taking life too seriously, following your inner joy.*

On purpose—*Recognizing and transcending inner boundaries, innovation, ambition, commitment to growth and change, combining unrelated things in new ways, creative solutions to apparent limitations, bringing order out of apparent chaos.*

Off purpose—*Conservatism, succumbing to judgments of others.*

TOWER

Growth challenge—*Breaking old patterns, releasing outdated roles, personal renovation, willingness to succeed.*

On purpose—*Fundamental change, breaking down defenses, destroying the old to make way for the new, desire for more beauty and authenticity, awareness of what's not working, disruption, dramatic self-improvement.*

Off purpose—*Being hard on yourself during change, stubborn resistance.*

STAR

Growth challenge—*Living your own truth, self-trust and respect, spiritual rebirth.*

On purpose—*Inexhaustible inspiration, self-esteem and confidence, spiritual regeneration, fully expressive, living personal truth, clarity of vision, desire to enlighten and raise consciousness.*

Off purpose—*Self-doubt, denying vision, withholding full involvement, creating or maintaining and image.*

MOON

Growth challenge—*Voluntary change, authentic expression, honoring and respecting your Self in all circumstances.*

On purpose—*Evolution, natural transformation, light in darkness, impelled from within, receptive, powerful, no tolerance for deception, flow with feelings.*

Off purpose—*Deception or being deceived, hiding, judging feelings and emotional states.*

SUN

Growth challenge—*Making inspirational connections, having "go for it" energy, creative exploration.*

On purpose—*Enlightenment, creativity and personal growth, natural generator, motivator, stimulator, joy, optimism, enthusiasm, vitality, idealistic, overcoming obstacles, successful, innovative.*

Off purpose—*Pessimism, seeing negativity, being at the effect.*

AEON / JUDGMENT

Growth challenge—*Being open to new activities, releasing judgments, sharing perceptions and ideas clearly.*

On purpose—*Final decisions concerning the past, wisdom from experience, awakening, sense of purpose, ability to see the whole picture, seeing without judgment, seeing beyond judgment, forgiveness.*

Off purpose—*Judging the past or present, being critical, holding grievances.*

UNIVERSE

Growth challenge—*Recognizing everything is available to you, experiencing no limitations, actualization of potential.*

On purpose—*Infinite potential, full expression of all aspects of the Self, completion, integration, dancing on limitations, renewal and regeneration, manifestation of Spirit on earth, active involvement.*

Off purpose—*Lack of gratitude, neediness, sadness.*

Enjoy The Journey

FOOL = *Start something new.*

MAGICIAN = *Clarity of thought and communication.*

HIGH PRIESTESS = *Develop intuition, resourcefulness, self-reliance*

EMPRESS = *Nurture creations, follow what has heart and meaning.*

EMPEROR = *Develop leadership and confidence, manifest vision for highest good.*

HEIROPHANT = *Strengthen inner voice, teaching/learning experiences.*

LOVERS = *Develop equality in relationships, perfect ability to work with others.*

CHARIOT = *Freedom, exploration, change, responsibility for choices.*

JUSTICE = *Build inner strength, stay balanced and centered, healing.*

HERMIT = *Experience mastery, follow inner conviction, lead by example.*

WHEEL OF FORTUNE = *Success, opportunities, endings and new beginnings.*

STRENGTH = *Tap into powerful inner resources, strength of passion and desires.*

HANGED MAN = *Letting go of the past and unnecessary attachments.*

DEATH/REBIRTH = *Transition, surrender to God, breaking limiting patterns.*

ART = *Creative activity, seeing new possibilities, being open-minded.*

DEVIL = *Recognize and transcend inner boundaries, new ways, follow inner joy.*

TOWER = *Awareness of what's not working, breaking old patterns, improvement.*

STAR = *Spiritual rebirth, clarity of vision, living your own truth.*

MOON = *Voluntary change, authentic expression, supporting true Self always.*

SUN = *Creative exploration, innovation, enlightenment, rebirth.*

AEON/JUDGMENT = *Final decision regarding past, forgiveness, no judgment.*

UNIVERSE = *Actualization of potential, manifestation of Spirit, no limits.*

At this point, you are willing to risk the loss of what you have, have accomplished and have been, and move on to what you can now become.

You return to the **FOOL**.

Robert Waldon, PhD, ND

Robert Waldon, ND, PhD

Natural Health Consultant
Specialized Kinesiologist
Ayurvedic Lifestyle Consultant
Touch For Health Instructor
Energetic Life Balancing Instructor
Reiki Master Teacher
B.A. in Psychology
Ph.D. in Holistic Health
ND in Natural Healing

Robert has doctorates in Naturopathy and Holistic Health as well as postgraduate degrees in Psychology, Education, Business and Finance and is a Certified Financial Planner. His well-rounded educational background and experience enrich his versatile style of presentation to educate and entertain, to inform and inspire. Robert's unique talent invites individuals to select effective tools and explore optimum possibilities leading to personal and professional fulfillment.

Robert spent the first four years of his career as an elementary school teacher. For the next ten years, he owned a successful Financial Planning firm designing Selective Executive Compensation and Benefit Plans for both private and Fortune 500 corporations. Since then, as founder and CEO of the Energetic Life Balancing Institute, Robert has trained and certified hundreds of professional practitioners across the U.S. and presented keynote programs for national business, health and educational conferences. He is a published author and has produced educational, motivational and training videos.

Robert designs and presents workshops and seminars nationwide, educating, inspiring and motivating individuals from a variety of professions and businesses. He empowers participants to achieve personal peak performance and increased levels of personal wellness and professional effectiveness.

Reunion Ministries
17664 Greenridge Road
Hidden Valley Lake, CA 95467

(800) 919-2392

Robert Waldon, PhD, ND

Robert@ReunionMinistries.org